LOST TOWERS

ALSO BY GREGORY A. BUTLER

DISUNITED BROTHERHOODS...race, racketeering and the fall of the New York construction unions [iUniverse Books, Lincoln, Nebraska, 2006]

LOST TOWERS

✦

...inside the World Trade Center cleanup

Gregory A. Butler

iUniverse, Inc.
New York Lincoln Shanghai

LOST TOWERS
...inside the World Trade Center cleanup

iUniverse books may be ordered through booksellers or by contacting:

iUniverse
2021 Pine Lake Road, Suite 100
Lincoln, NE 68512
www.iuniverse.com
1-800-Authors (1-800-288-4677)

The views expressed herein are the sole responsibility of the author and do not necessarily reflect the views of iUniverse or it's affiliates.

ISBN-13: 978-0-595-40919-8 (pbk)
ISBN-13: 978-0-595-85282-6 (ebk)
ISBN-10: 0-595-40919-9 (pbk)
ISBN-10: 0-595-85282-3 (ebk)

Printed in the United States of America

Contents

ACKNOWEDGEMENTS

This is my second foray into the wonderful world of publishing…and it's a long way from carrying a toolbag to sitting in front of the keyboard…

I would never have attempted to write this book if I hadn't published my first work "DISUNITED BROTHERHOODS…race, racketeering and the fall of the New York construction unions" [iUniverse Books, 2006]…

That work was many years in the making…and not just the 2 years it took to write it, but the years of learning that it took to make me capable of putting pen to paper on that kind of scale…

So, I've got to take a brief pause, and thank all the folks who, in one way or another, made my first book possible—my mom, Peggy Butler, my dad, the late Ronald C. Butler, my brother, the late Chris Butler, Elissa K. West, Kevin Mercadel, Carlos R. Dufflar, Dr Ed Johnson, Angel Martinez, Kazembe Balagon, Kwame Madhi, Kenny Chesney, Ebony La Brew, Marilyn P. "Marty" Small, Jim McGuire, La Verne Byners, Harvey Shulman, Doreen Gay, Mike Daly, Tommy Higgins, Cynthia "Torie" Aldrich, Kevin Spillane, Karol Lobb, Bob Del Rossi, Bob Cadet, Walter Marano, Dwana Lateen Pray, Tim Wheeler, the late Fred "Hy Clymer" Gabory, Jason Rabinowitz, Bob Fitch, Noble Bratton, Dr Immanuel "Manny" Ness, Sander Hicks, Ken Nash, Mimi Rosenberg and Taiisha Herrera…

I'd also like to thank Phil Whitmarsh, Ron Amack and the rest of the crew out at iUniverse Books in fabulous Lincoln, Nebraska…without your world class typesetting, graphic design and printing, and your access to amazon.com and barnesandnoble.com, neither my first book nor this one would be possible…

Finally, I'd like to thank everybody that ever spoke to me about Ground Zero, on or off the record…nobody should have to see what you all saw down there…and hopefully one day we'll live in a world where nobody will…

INTRODUCTION

♦

Collapse Zone

On a bright Tuesday morning in September 2001, most New Yorkers could never have imagined that our city would be subject to a full scale terrorist attack...

After all, that's the kind of stuff that happens in other countries, far away tragedies that happen to people who don't look like us...fuzzy video images of distant horrors that flicker across the screen of the CNN newscast...

That couldn't happen here in the self-proclaimed "capital of the world", right???

Well, it could...and it did...

And the raiders couldn't have picked a more symbolic target...

The seven towers of the World Trade Center were not only the City of New York's most prominent landmark, they also represented the global economic power of Wall Street and Corporate America

And not just symbolically...

Some of the nation's leading financial firms—companies like Solomon Smith Barney, Morgan Stanley Dean Whitter, Cantor Fitzgerald and the Aon Corporation—ran their Wall Street operations out of the towers...

Just about every other major bank and brokerage house on the planet had offices there too

Many of the city's leading law firms had their offices in the towers—for the lawyers, the towers were doubly convenient—the WTC was within walking distance of all of the major courthouses in Manhattan and the offices of most of their major corporate clients...

Also, the US Customs Service processed all of the tariffs collected from international commercial traffic through the Port of New York in the complex—they actually had their own building, Tower 6…

There were other major tenants too—Blue Cross/Blue Shield of Greater New York ran it's claims processing, provider relations and customer service operations out of the towers

The complex also housed the headquarters of the Port Authority of New York and New Jersey—the corporation jointly owned by the states of New York and New Jersey that ran New York City's bustling air and sea ports, bus terminals, industrial parks and the PATH Train—the little subway system that linked Manhattan and Jersey City…

The Port Authority had been the complex's landlord from the time of their completion in 1972 right up to just 11 days before the attacks (when they leased the towers for 99 years to Silverstein Properties, a firm owned by real estate billionare Larry Silverstein)

The towers also housed the Commodity Exchange, where much of the world's gold, silver and oil are traded…

That last item perhaps explains why the terrorists targeted the towers—after all, they were exiles from Saudi Arabia, a petroleum rich state who's energy resources, government and economy are completely American controlled—and their country's oil was bought and sold on the trading floors of the WTC…

Al-Qaeda [Arabic for "the base"], the movement to which the attackers belonged, sought to end American corporate control of their kingdom and it's oil resources, by any means necessary…

In their minds, what better way was there to do this than to blow up the headquarters of the foreign financiers who dominated their homeland (even if it meant killing a whole bunch of innocent civilians in the process)???

That was the ugly logic behind their murderous attack on the trade center…

The terrorist attack on the World Trade Center was an extraordinary event in a number of other ways as well…

First and foremost it was the first foreign military attack on the City of New York since the British Navy shelled Battery Park during theWar of 1812…

That attack took the form of the first successful airliner hijacking in the United States in 17 years…

That attack was also the first coordinated multiple aircraft hijacking ever in this country, (and only the second simultaneous 4 plane hijacking in history—the only other one was in Jordan in September 1970)

And the first time anybody in the world ever used commercial airliners full of innocent people as kamikaze attack aircraft

And, in reaction to the hijacking, the Federal Aviation Administration grounded every single civillian aircraft in the country, for the first time in American history…

Those four hijackings led to the largest deployment in the history of the New York Fire Department—the dispatchers stopped counting alarms when they got to 40—over 1,200 firefighters responded…and 343 never left the WTC alive (the largest loss of life in the history of the FDNY)…

The fall of the two 110 story towers was the largest building collapse in the history of the world, and touched off the longest fire in New York City history—the rubble didn't stop burning for almost 4 months…

The site of the ruined World Trade Center (which came to be known as "Ground Zero", a name given the site by television reporters in the early afternoon of Tuesday, September 11—to the workers involved it was known as "the pit") also became the largest demolition job in New York City history.

The damaged but still standing buildings surrounding the pit, on the perimiter of the Ground Zero security zone, also became one of the largest renovation jobs in city history as well (with, among other repairs, over 12,000 windows replaced).

During the peak of the Ground Zero job, at any given time there were over 3,000 workers employed in and around Ground Zero, and another 3,000 teamsters trucking debris out of the site…

Alongside the 35,000 military personnel, federal, state and local civil servants who were at Ground Zero at some point, there were approximately 40,000 civilians in the site…

About 8,000 men and women worked in the pit at some point, and at least 32,000 other workers (including this writer) were employed in the security zone at least one day during the 9 month recovery operation.

Those civilian workers (who are the focus of this book) had a wide range of skill levels, from highly trained ironworkers, operating engineers and hazardous materials laborers to immigrant day laborers and janitors with zero safety training and 99 cent store dust masks

Their working conditions varied radically too…from virtually normal jobsites with regular workdays in the buildings on the edge of the pit to "7/12's" [seven day workweeks and twelve hour shifts] in the debris and human remains-filled foundation hole that had once been two of the tallest buildings on the planet…

But, no matter what part of the site workers were on, the attitude was the same—get the job done as quickly as possible…

This was ESPECIALLY true in the pit, where workers had the extra special responsibility of guaranteeing a decent burial to the 2,900+ murder victims who's dismembered bodies were entombed in the wreckage…

Workers were willing to take extraordinary risks, and expose themselves to extreme danger to life and limb…

And that willingness to sacrifice and dedication to duty was throughly abused by the financial interests that had a money stake in rebuilding rentable floor space over the devestated site as quickly as possible…crime scene investigation, body recovery and worker safety be damned…

Worse yet, the unions to which most Ground Zero workers belonged stood idly by and let it happen…in the name of patriotism…

This job was a deathtrap…

Even during the recovery operation, over 5,400 workers got hurt…

Today, 5 years after the towers fell, we're seeing the first of the long term health effects...

As of this writing (in late July 2006), there are at least 57 workers dead, and more than 12,000 sick with various illnesses (including something called "World Trade Center Cough"—a disease that didn't even exist prior to 9/11)...

And that's not even tallying the psychological casualties—the many Ground Zero workers still bedeveled by nightmares and post-traumatic stress from the horrors they saw in the pit...

The Ground Zero site was a place of great bravery and heroism...and terrible villany and greed...

Here is that story...

1

"...code 10–60" from World Trade Center to Ground Zero (September 11, 2001)

"...remain in your seats, we are returning to the airport. Don't do anything stupid"

Those were the last words that the Federal Aviation Administration air traffic controllers at Boston's Logan International Airport ever heard from the cockpit of American Airlines Flight 11, a Boeing 767 jumbo jet that had been flying non stop to Los Angeles until it disappeared from the radar scopes shortly after take-off...

Needless to say, the speaker was NOT the pilot...

It was an Egyptian-born engineer, licensed pilot and professional terrorist from Hamburg, Germany by the name of Mohammad Atta

Along with 4 other members of a Saudi Arabian-exile terrorist group called al-Qaeda ["the base"], Atta had just commandeered the aircraft, killing both pilots and a passenger and severely injuring two flight attendants in the process...

Their weapons?

Swiss Army knives the air pirates had snuck aboard the plane...

Atta was actually trying to speak to the passengers...apparently he pushed the wrong button and radioed the tower...

The air traffic controllers, throughly disturbed by that message, radioed United Airlines Flight 175, another Boeing 767 bound non stop for Los Angeles, asking the pilots if they could check on Flight 11...

Unfortunately, those crewmen had already been murdered by the time their plane was contacted...

The killers, Marwan al-Shehhi and his brother Alawal, Mohammad Atta's cousins from the Emirate of Dubai, were also engineers, licensed pilots and full time terrorists...

And the brothers al-Shehhi, along with 3 other hijackers, were in league with Atta and his men...and 9 other al-Qaeda "undercover brothers" aboard 2 other planes (American Airlines Flight 77 out of Dulles Airport and United Airlines Flight 93 out of Newark)...

These 19 professional killers were carrying out what their organization would call a "martyrdom operation"...

Internally within al-Qaeda this particular mission was codenamed "Bojinka"...

In the dialect of Arabic spoken in Saudi Arabia, that means "large explosion"...

After Atta and the al-Shehhi brothers had disabled the plane's transponders, thus making the big jumbo jets unidentifiable to the computers of the FAA and the Air National Guard, flights11 and 175 changed course far away from their authorized paths...

They followed slightly different routes—Atta went straight down the Hudson River, the al-Shehhi's flew low and fast over Long Island Sound, across the Bronx, New Jersey and Lower New York Bay, but they both had the same destination...the World Trade Center...

As the lead kamikaze plane zoomed southwards towards New York City, rapidly diving from 37,000 feet to 1,000, flight attendants Betty Ong and Madeline Amy Sweeney were huddled near the rear of the jumbo jet with the terrified passengers and their two badly wounded co-workers...

Seperately, the two airline workers surrupticiously grabbed Verizon airfones...

Independently of each other, both Ong and Sweeney gave running commentaries on the lethal air piracy to their American Airlines fight attendant supervisors

On it's way to oblivion, Flight 11 passed about rooftop height over the Trump Riverside South development on Manhattan's West Side...

A concrete gang working for Northside Construction were just finishing up the roof of the 4th luxury hirse apartment building in that complex on that fateful Tuesday morning...

3rd year apprentice cement mason Kenneth Chesney had just gotten back with the coffee order...

As the guys sat down to break "we saw this plane going down the Hudson on the New Jersey side—it was right above the river practically."

"It could have hit the top of the building—it seemed like it was 50 feet above us. It was really fucking scary...I've never seen a plane that big that close going that fast..."

"We thought they were going to crash into the water...and it goes on down the Hudson—we thought it was going out to sea to ditch, in the bay or something..."

"Then we started seeing the black smoke coming from the World Trade Center..."

At that very moment, flight attendant Sweeney phoned her last words to her supervisor at Logan Airport "I see water and buildings...Oh my God!!! Oh my God!!!"

Then the line went dead...

It was 8:46AM, Eastern Standard Time...

Within less than 2 hours, the buildings that had been a symbol of New York City for the previous 29 years would be a pile of smoldering rubble...

As the first plane hit, carpenter foreman Roger Lee and several other Port Authority tradespeople were setting up for the last lunchtime concert of the summer in Austin J. Tobin Plaza, the large open square between Towers 1 and 2...

"We were hit by a shower of broken glass…The stagehand foreman got cut open—his guts were spilling out—he bled to death in my arms…"

Lee got the Port Authority police to take care of his murdered co-worker, and then he hastily organized an evacuation of the rest of the crew out of the WTC complex…

Two blocks away at 2 Washington St, the offices of the Child Support Enforcement Unit of the NYC Adminstration for Children's Services, caseworker/enforcement agent Fady Mitchell was preparing to handle the day's deadbeat dad wage garnisheements when a loud noise and a bright flash from outside distracted her…

"We were inside working when the first plane hit…I didn't see the plane, but I saw this big orange fireball…"

Sixteen minutes later, the al-Shehhi brothers, at the controls of United Airlines Flight 175, roared about 600 feet over the building where Mitchell and her fellow ACS agents were looking out the windows at the smoke consuming the top of WTC Tower 1…

"Then somebody said 'a second plane hit!!!'…"

As the jumbo jet tore into the side of WTC Tower 2 "our whole building shook and then all the fire alarms went off and everybody was screaming and hollering…and then we ran outside, down the stairs, two at a time…"

While Lee and Mitchell were getting a front row seat view of the carnage, a couple million New Yorkers (along with hundreds of millions around the world) saw the unfolding horrorshow live on TV…

This writer had just finished voting in the primary elections that day…

I had the day off from work—ironically enough, I'd spent much of the early part of 2001 as the carpenter shop steward for Trinity Carpentry & Systems Installation, a furniture contractor installing desks in WTC Tower 1, 49th Floor—the client, Dai Ichi Kangyo Bank, was running the job in phases and we were supposed to go back on Thursday, September 13…

As I turned on the city's 24 hour all news channel, New York 1, the station's normally cheerful morning anchor Pat Kiernan was obviously distraught as he narrated live footage of the burning Tower 1 being filmed from atop the studio…

If that wasn't a hard enough job for Kiernan, then fate handed him the hellish task of giving what amounted to a live play-by-play account of the kamikaze attack by Flight 175's murderous hijackers…as what looked to TV viewers like a little dot raced from the upper right hand of the screen and disappeared into the back of Tower 2—soon to be replaced by an awful orange fireball…

Within moments, New York 1's computers had enhanced the image of that little black dot…it was clear this was a commercial aircraft, painted in the blue, grey and red color scheme of United Airlines…and that there must have been innocents trapped aboard the jet as it was transformed into a flying bomb…

Soon, every TV station in New York became "WTC-TV"…and that would be the only program on for the next 3 days…

Eric Josephson, a New York City Transit trackworker and Transport Workers Union local 100 shop steward, was one of the viewers…

He'd started his day unloading work trains at the Authority's Westchester Square railroad yard in the Bronx when "a conductor told me (about the first plane hitting the tower) so I went to the crew room—they usually have TVs in the crew rooms—and everybody was saying 'what the hell is this!?! It's got to be terrorists!!!'"

"I was a little slow on the uptake on that—I thought it had to be a government, it was too organized—I didn't know about the hijackings or the planes yet…"

After the second plane was crashed "…there was no work…people were speculating, I was speculating…"

As Josephson and his co-workers speculated, NYC Transit train operator Harry Harrington sprang into action…

He was at the controls of a Brooklyn-bound R train at the Rector Street Station, just underneath two of the lowrise WTC buildings, Towers 4 and 5, and in the shadow of Tower 2. He hastily evacuated his train's passengers, along with his conductor and the station agents and cleaners who worked on the platforms…

Ironically, Harrington, like many New Yorkers, just happens to be a Sikh…

Despite the fact that a member of their religion was one of the first "heroes of Ground Zero" many Sikhs would be harassed, and even physically attacked, in the days following the air raid—solely because they wear turbans, and in the eyes of some enraged racists they "looked like Muslims" (even though they are not)

In reaction to those bias crimes, the Authority would try and force Harrington and other Sikh transit workers to remove their turbans during working hours (rather than trying to defend them from being assaulted and abused)

As train operator Harrington dispersed his passengers out onto Church St, others rushed down to the WTC site…

John McGrail, the safety director at the New York City District Council of Carpenters Labor Technical College, grabbed his first aid kit and, along with several other staffers, took off on foot from the school's Hudson Street classrooms the one mile down to the World Trade Center…

Laborer Pete Dinuzzo left his jobsite, and rushed to the scene…Dinuzzo, a Navy veteran and longtime union activist, was anxious to help out the best he could…

They would be among the first of the thousands of New York construction workers who would travel to the site to aid the living (and, ultimately, recover the dead)…

Along with the volunteers, the city's professional emergency workers rushed to the site…

The New York City Fire Department, for the first time in it's history, recalled every single off duty firefighter to work…

The department called in every available firetruck and ambulance, even asking for aid from departments across the river in New Jersey and out in Long Island…It was the FDNY's biggest incident response ever…

The World Trade Center, which housed the headquarters of the Port Authority of New York & New Jersey, was protected by the Authority's in house law enforcement agency, the Port Authority Police Department…

The PAPD called in every available officer (some went to the towers, others equipped themselves with machine guns, kevlar helmets and bulletproof vests and went to secure the city's airports against a possible second wave of hijackings)...

The NYPD and just about every other law enforcement agency in the city sent every cop they could find to the scene as well

Many officers deserted their posts in other parts of the city to get down to the towers and help out—including many of the cops on desk duty at One Police Plaza, the nearby NYPD headquarters...

They faced a hellish scene when they arrived...the top of Tower 1 and the middle of Tower 2 were completely in flames, and burning pieces of the doomed aircraft had set fire to Tower 7, the Deutsche Bank Building and 90 West Street.

Unfortunately for the first responders, the main emergency incident command post in the city, Mayor Rudolph Giuliani's "bunker", just happened to be inside Tower 7, on the 16th floor...

In a bit of cosmicly bad luck, one of the engines of Flight 175 had flown through Tower 2 and actually rammed right into the bunker...

Worse yet, the white-hot GE turbofan, still propelling itself forward at 600 mph despite being severed from it's aircraft, hit the 42,000 gallon diesel fuel tank that served the bunker's generator...

This not only wrecked the bunker, but set fire to the rest of the 50 story building as well...

Incidentally, maintaining a fuel tank, of any size, in an office building is in violation of both the New York City Building Code and the New York City Fire Code...let alone having that much diesel fuel around that much combustible paper and furniture

But, since the generator system served an NYC Office of Emergency Management command post, it was considered exempt...

Incidentally, since the WTC complex as a whole was owned by the Port Authority, there were many aspects of the towers construction that were less than building code compliant—including the relatively weak open web truss-style steel beams that supported the floor decks in Towers 1 and 2—but, due to the sovereign immunity the bi-state corporation claimed, the PA had never been called to account for these violations…

Back across the street in the WTC, many folks were trapped above the flames in the two hirise towers…

In the case of Tower 1, 80 workers and 160 customers in the Windows on the World restaurant, along with several hundred office workers in the upper floors of the towers, were trapped with no way out, since Flight 11 had destroyed all 3 emergency stairways…

Or, actually, they had one way out…

Out the windows…

The folks in the upper floors of Tower 1 had a Gary Gilmore choice—they would surely die, but they got to choose how—quickly by falling or slowly by smoke and heat…

About 200 people took the fast way out…

Fady Mitchell and her co-workers got to see this close up "…I thought it was paper flying down…then I realized it was people!!!"

The viewers at home got to see the morbid display too—or at least some of them did…

New York's English language TV stations cut away to distant shots when folks started free falling out the windows…the Spanish stations did closeups on the victims as they fell to earth…(including a husband and wife who jumped hand-in-hand)…

So many folks leaped it actually became a safety hazard for the 20,000+ people escaping the towers—and the rescue workers aiding them (several firefighters—including the FDNY's chief chaplain Rev Mychal Judge—were killed when people landed on them)

They were among the first firefighters to die that day—but unfortunately they would not be the last…

This air attack had happened at the height of New York's rush hour—many of the 500,000 men and women who worked in the area were still on their way to work at the time of the attacks...

Khadija Lawrence, a customer service rep for stock photo agency Getty Images, was one of them..."I came out of the train station and there was mad people just standin there—and then I saw the twin towers was burnin!!! some guy said 'two planes crashed into the buildings'...and we were just standin there watchin them burn...".

At the time, many folks, firefighter and civilian alike, actually thought the towers would survive this disaster, despite the obvious massive structural damage.

Which really isn't that surprising...many New Yorkers had always thought of the twin towers as indestructable...when they were built, it had been claimed that they could withstand a nuclear bomb blast...and a lot of us actually believed that...

Problem was, that really wasn't true...actually, the steel structure of the WTC towers was weaker than the average hirise building...we'd find that out the hard way that morning...

Fady Mitchell recalls "you know, it's stupid...I saw the firemen go in there—you know the ones that went in and never came out??? and I thought they were going to put it out...Isn't it stupid??? I really thought they were going to put the fire out..."

Unfortunately, they did not...

By 10:02AM, Tower 2 could no longer withstand the damage it had sustained, and it failed...

Khadija Lawrence was close enough to actually hear the bolts on the steel beams pop "they sounded like gunshots..."

This was the begining of the biggest building collapse in human history...

As it fell, pieces of Tower 2 ripped a 15 story hole in the side of the Deutsche Bank Building, crushed the upper floors of the Marriott World Trade Center Hotel, crushed the roof of WTC Tower 4, caved in the 1 train subway tunnel and the Cortlandt St station underneath Austin J. Tobin Plaza, sent steel beams hurtling into the R train tunnel and the Rector St station under Church St, filled the PATH train station with rubble, packed the shopping mall beneath the towers with hundreds of tons of debris and sent out a massive wave of concrete dust...

Mitchell and her co-workers, a scant two blocks from the lost tower, were caught right in the thick of it "we were out in the park—and when that first building went down the whole island was covered in smoke—we thought we were going to suffocate—everybody was screaming and hollering...we ran to the ferry...we thought we were going to die..."

The ACS workers boarded the last regularly scheduled Staten Island Ferry to leave Manhattan that day...and became the first of over 300,000 Lower Manhattan workers evacuated by boat from the scene (the biggest sea evacuation since the British Army's retreat from France in May 1940)...

Mitchell would spend the night in the ferry terminal on the Staten Island side, unable to return to her home in Queens until late the next day...

Although they were dust-covered, tired and emotionally exhausted, the boat evacuees were very lucky to be alive...many of the attack's victims had died in the collapse of Tower 2—including much of the FDNY's high command...

They had set up their command post too close...the fire chiefs had wanted to maintain some order amid the hundreds of random firefighters who'd shown up at the scene, so they thought they had to be very close to the action...

Their idea had it's merits—the chiefs were able to provide a measure of coordination and discipline to the chaotic fireground, and the officers were able to successfully manage the evacuation of the 20,000+ workers who were in the towers (the largest evacuation ever carried out by any fire department in the world)...

But that decision also placed the command post well within the collapse zone—a fatal mistake, as it turned out...

Meanwhile, people all over the city saw the growing cloud emerging over Lower Manhattan—including trackworker Eric Josephson up in the Northeast Bronx "I went out to Westchester Square—you used to be able to see the World Trade Center from there, kinda fuzzy but you could see it—there was just a big column of this beige smoke—very eerie and disturbing..."

Josephson was anxious to get added to one of the many track gangs being rushed downtown to assess the damage to the three subway tunnels running under what had been the World Trade Center (a place the TV newscasters had already begun calling "Ground Zero")...

But, there was a problem...

Josephson was a union militant, a socialist and a constant thorn in the side of New York City Transit management—so they didn't want him anywhere near this job...despite his 17 years of experience as a trackworker and his extensive safety training...

He would end up having to go down there on his own time, as a volunteer...

Meanwhile, some of the other terrorists had succeeded in their homicidal "martyrdom operations" (American Airlines Flight 77 had been rammed into the Pentagon, wrecking 1/5th of the US Department of Defense headquarters) while others were defeated by a revolt of the hijacking victims (United Airlines Flight 93's passengers took the plane back—and saved the US Capitol by crashing the Boeing 757 into a field in rural Pennsylvania)...

Tower 1 wasn't long for this world—it followed it's twin into history at 10:30 AM...

The doomed skyscraper cut the US Customs House at Tower 6 in half, sent debris showering into the Crystal Pavilion on the other side of West St in the World Financial Center, crushed the Vesey St pedestrian overpass (killing numerous firefighters and civilians huddled underneath), flooded West St with rubble, filled the rest of the WTC shopping mall with debris, ripped a huge hole in the side of the American Express Tower (killing 11 workers in that building in the process) and tore off large sections of the exterior wall of the Verizon building...

That building housed 10% of all the phone lines in New York City—the damage sustained in the collapse cut off landline phone service to a huge section of Lower Manhattan...

Tower 1's fall sent another huge blast of dust and smoke across Lower Manhattan, enveloping everything from Canal St down to the tip of the borough for a second time...

A number of fleeing office workers actually died of athsma attacks caused by the great noxious cloud…

Meanwhile, laborer Pete Dinuzzo had already arrived on the scene—he would be one of the first of many volunteers—he actualy got hit by a piece of Tower 1 as it fell—a metal panel from the exterior skin of the tower smacked him across the back…but Dinuzzo was undeterred, and immediately set about the task of helping the rescue operation…

John McGrail's team from the Carpenters Union health & safety department had been caught over in Battery Park City by the smoke cloud…but they made it to the hastily set up first aid station at the Staten Island ferry terminal…

Upon seeing that there were few injured people there needing their assistance (basically, the only folks who made it out of the WTC were those who were able to walk…most of the folks who'd suffered serious injuries in the towers died when the buildings fell) the Carpenters Union safety guys went into the collapse zone…

Other construction workers across the city would soon follow in McGrail and Dinuzzo's footsteps…in Eric Josephson's words "…they saw that this was their responsibility…it came naturally to them to handle this…"

Or, to be totally honest, SOME construction workers saw that this was their responsibility

On Kenneth Chesney's jobsite, many of the workers joined the sea of other New Yorkers fleeing the scene of the disaster…

"Willie said 'something's going on! We're under attack!'—he's in the defensive mindset, being an ex-soldier—'we're all going to get blown up—I'm going home to be with my family, to protect my wife and kids'—he knew something big is going on—he just fuckin left the site—'this will be my last minutes on Earth, I want to be with my family, not you guys!!!'"

Other guys on Northside Construction's crew at Trump Riverside South felt differently "about a third of the guys decided to go down and help out…"

But, even then, some of the workers, in particular the older European immigrants who'd seen World War II air raids up close and personal, had serious reservations about going to Ground Zero

"We were in the shanty—me, my foreman Vinny, Tony, and some of the other older Italian guys—packing up our shit and getting ready to leave"

"Some carpenter poked his head in 'a bunch of us are going down to help out—if you want to join us come on…'"

"Vinny said 'Don't be stupid, don't go down there—all those guys are going to be sick or dead in 10 years…all that dust and material in the air…stay away, stay as far away as possible!!!!'"

As it turns out, that old Italian cement mason foreman's prediction was right on the money (as we'll see later in this book)

The carpenters didn't listen to Vinny…their desire to help outweighed any concern for their personal safety…but Chesney and the other masons did…"I had no intention of going anywhere near—who knows how many planes or bombs they had??? besides the environmental hazards…"

Before fleeing the site, Chesney paused with a few other tradespeople to watch the now forever changed skyline "me and these Irish laborers went down to this brand new pier that Trump built on the river—they had binoculars—by then the towers were down…we saw all the debris and smoke…"

They were surrounded by traumatized New Yorkers who were also taking in the horriffic scene "there were all kinds of people in the park—it was real quiet—some people talking low, others crying and hugging and stuff…"

And then the long trek home began…

"I had to walk—lucky I didn't carry too many tools that day—I had to walk all the way to 138th St—subways shut down, no cabs, a few cars…some covered with inch thick dust—they must have come from downtown…"

"They were like cattle, man, just walking up Broadway for as far as you could see…"

"People were offering $ 20 or $ 30 just to ride in the back of a truck…"

"By 59th St any car that had extra space was full—but the traffic was so bad you might as well have walked…"

"I've never seen so many people walking in my life—there must have been millions of them—some of these people had come all the way from downtown and had to go all the way to the Bronx…"

Khadija Lawrence was one of those unfortunate folks—with the 4 and 5 trains knocked out, she had to travel on foot all the way up to her apartment on East 141st St, a distance of about 8 miles…

Meanwhile, elements of the 101st Cavalry Regiment, 42nd "Rainbow" Infantry Division, New York State National Guard, had arrived on scene, to enforce the security zone that Mayor Giuliani had ordered imposed in Lower Manhattan…

There were two layers of military/police checkpoints—one at 14th St, and the other at Canal St—staffed by a composite crew of cops, federal agents and soldiers…

NYPD and Port Authority cops, reinforced by police officers from Nassau County and other nearby suburbs, as well as federal agents and national guard troops, also sealed off the major river crossings leading to Lower Manhattan—the Holland and Brooklyn Battery tunnels, and the Brooklyn, Manhattan and Williamsburg bridges

On the East Side, this meant there were no river crossings below the Queens Midtown Tunnel at 34th St—on the West Side, it was impossible to cross the Hudson below the Lincoln Tunnel on 39th St…

Even there, and on every other bridge or tunnel, there were police checkpoints, and all vehicles (in particular white trucks and vans—a popular vehicle type used by carbombers around the world) were subject to immediate warantless search…

Between 14th and Canal, in the Security Zone, only residents were allowed—below Canal St was the 'Frozen Zone'—where everybody had to evacuate immediately…

New York City's subway system also was cut in half…

14th St was the last stop for all downtown service and Manhattan-bound trains terminated in Downtown Brooklyn, basically dividing the city in two…

The mayor also cancelled the primary elections that had been going on that day…

Giuliani also briefly considered cancelling the November general elections as well—and extending his soon to expire second term of office for another two years…

Cooler heads soon prevailed, and that undemocratic plan was immediately abandoned…

Meanwhile, Seven World Trade Center, the 50 story office tower across the street from the rest of the complex, joined it's namesake buildings as a pile of rubble…

The fires fueled by Mayor Giuliani's 42,000 gallon diesel fuel tank had weakened the structural steel, and it collapsed 10 hours after the attacks…

On the way down, Seven World Trade destroyed the Con Edison electrical substation located in it's basement, plunging much of Lower Manhattan into darkness, and it also wrecked Fitterman Hall, a newly built wing of the Borough of Manhattan Community College that had just had it's grand opening a few days before the attacks…

As Tower 7 fell, a sense of trauma and panic beset the city…

In the plaza on the south end of Union Square Park, on the edge of the northernmost set of National Guard checkpoints on 14th St, relatives of World Trade Center workers who hadn't come home began to gather…

Many of them had hastily made missing person posters, with photographs and hand scrawled information, and taped them up around the southern edge of the park…soon the posters spread up and down 14th St, from river to river…

Almost all of those posters mentioned the missing loved one's employer, and what floor they worked on…

As it happened, a lot of those folks worked on the higher floors—WTC 1 102nd Floor, WTC 2 78th Floor, ect…and, in the coming days it would be all too clear exactly what had happened to these luckless individuals…

At that point, nobody knew exactly how many folks had died…amazingly high numbers were floating around—Mayor Giuliani, in one of his many press conferences, speculated that as many as 20,000 had perished…

It's not surprising the early estimates were so high…an awful lot of folks used to work in the towers…

50,000+ white collar workers had their desks in the complex…

The buildings were maintained by over 1,500 blue collar workers…

More than 1,000 workers staffed the stores and restaurants…

400 Port Authority cops and private security guards protected the 7 buildings…

Every day several hundred truck drivers, messengers, restaurant delivery workers, job applicants, clients and other visitors came into the towers…

And several dozen homeless people lived in the shopping mall and the 3 subway stations beneath the buildings…

In those early confused hours, nobody really knew how many people had gotten out alive, since a lot of the evacuated workers were still walking home or had been dropped off by boat in Staten Island or New Jersey…

And it wasn't like they could phone home…the high volume of calls and the loss of the switchgear at the Verizon building on Vesey St made it almost impossible to get a dial tone, either on a landline or a cell…

Nor could the fire chiefs and Port Authority police officers who'd run the evacuation confirm how many folks they'd saved—since they were dead beneath the ruins…

So nobody really knew how many folks had even been in the buildings when they got hit, let alone how many had actually escaped the fallen towers…

Or, for that matter, how many were still living, but trapped amid the twisted steel…

Worse yet, the entity that ran the WTC, the Port Authority, was not in any condition to lead any effective rescue mission…

Many top Port Authority managers, including the authority's president, had been killed in the collapse...and the few still living PA executives had no place to command from, since their headquarters had been in the towers...

As for the City of New York, Mayor Giuliani and Police Commissioner Bernard Kerik were very very very busy giving press conferences and getting themselves on the front pages of Wednesday's newspapers...

After all, they both had political ambitions—(Giuliani actually wanted to be the next President of the United States—an ambition he maintains to this very day) and this was a once-in-a-lifetime opportunity for them to get national media exposure...

And it worked—at least for Giuliani, who is still presented to this very day by the media as "the hero of 9/11" even though he didn't rescue one survivor, find the body of one victim or remove even one pound of rubble...

It didn't go over nearly so well for Kerik—the former bodyguard for the King of Saudi Arabia's meteoric rise to the top after 9/11 would later be derailed by the exposure, several years later, of his alleged ties to the Gambino crime family

Investigators would eventually find that the commissioner had $ 200,000 in renovations to his Bronx apartment done by Interstate Industrial, a drywall contractor allegedly under the protection of the Gambino family...

This work was done free of charge—in return for which Kerik, allegedly, helped the company get cleared to do casino construction in New Jersey...

As Rudy and Bernie cynically used the bodies of 2,900 murdered New Yorkers as a platform to get themselves on the evening news, there were lower ranking city officials who specifically dealt with construction matters who were actually getting involved with the disaster in a more serious way...

Unfortunately, they weren't really that focused on the death and destruction...they had other things on their minds...

Deputy Mayor Rudy Washington, NYC Department of Design and Construction Commissioner Kenneth Holden and NYC DDC Deputy Commissioner Michael Burton had all been construction industry executives before they became city officials...

And they were quite busy handing out contracts for Ground Zero demolition work and debris hauling…

There was no attempt to hand out these contracts on a competitively bid basis…

Instead, they were handshake deals, with companies hand-picked by Washington, Holden and Burton being given these jobs with other firms not even given the opportunity to make offers…

There were no set fees in these contracts either…the contractors would be paid "on T & M"—Time and Materials—that is, the contractors would tell the city how much they'd paid for labor and supplies, and the city would cut a check…

Of course, these type of contracts are prone to abuse…it's easy for contractors to line their pockets by lying about their expenses…which is why it's almost unheard of for a job this big to be bid out this way…

By a really funny coincidence, many of the contractors who won these sweetheart deals just happened to have ties to the Deputy Mayor and/or the two DDC executives…

I wonder how that happened???

They also had to take care of one Larry Silverstein, the billionare real estate developer who owned Seven World Trade Center, and who had just signed a 99 year lease on the other 6 towers with the Port Authority on September 1, 2001…

Silverstein had agreed to pay the Port Authority $ 1.2 million dollars a month for the 6 towers every month for the next century

Unfortunately for him, he had to pay even if the 15 million square feet of office space in the towers became unrentable—as, of course, it presently had…

So, even as the towers burned and live survivors and the unburied dead lay beneath twisted rubble, Mr Silverstein was already planning the "new" World Trade Center to be built atop the ashes of the old…

According to anonymous sources in the New York District Council of Carpenters, the initial planning of the 4 towers that would replace the 7 destroyed buildings had already begun within hours of the bombing…

Silverstein was already having his lawyers fill out the claim forms for the $ 3.3 billion dollars in insurance policies he had on the towers…

Which would be perfectly understandable…except for the way those forms got filled out…

In an astonishing act of greed, venality and, dare I say it, the moral equivilent of looting, Silverstein made two claims on each policy—in other words, he asked for $ 6.6 billion in payments on $ 3,300,000,000 in policies…

The excuse was, it was two planes, so it was two incidents, so Mr Silverstein should get paid twice…

Despite the fact that this was, essentially, a form of insurance fraud, the City supported Mr Silverstein every step of the way in this apalling act of corporate greed (and continues to back him up to this day)…

Even amid the carnage of the day, the smoke darkened streets filled with American war refugees, the priorities were clear…

Bottom line, there was money involved, quite a lot of it…and, in the minds of these guys, dividing up the ocean of government aid and insurance settlements soon to flood the former WTC site mattered a whole lot more than rescuing trapped victims or recovering the deceased…

A lot of this wheeling and dealing apparently happend at the Ground Zero site itself, since Washington, Holden and Burton all had quickly set up temporary offices near the site, in the now deserted classrooms of PS 89, an elementary school up on Chambers Street…

The school was just a short walk from Ground Zero…

Just a couple blocks south of those bright cheerful rooms decorated with kids drawings, where questionable business arrangements were being hammered out by grown men in suits uncomfortably squeezed into kindergarden student's desks, a Port Authority worker named Genelle Guzman lay entombed in the ruins of a staircase, trapped next to the bodies of two dead firemen…

The 31 year old clerk happened to be pregnant…and both her legs had been broken in the collapse…but she was still alive, awaiting rescue, in the dark, with no food or water…

Her fate probably didn't matter that much to the Deputy Mayor, the Commissioner and the Deputy Commissioner, as they hammered out big money deals amid blackboards and children's books, after all, what's more important, a secretary's life or a couple billion dollars in government contracts??

It wasn't like Washington, Holden or Burton bore Guzman, or any of the other trapped survivors, any personal ill will—it was just that there was so much money involved, and that was far more important than a few workers slowly dying in the dark under heaps of rubble that had once been their offices…

Luckily for Guzman, there were people on the site who weren't blinded by avarice, and who actually gave a damn about the fate of her and the others trapped in the debris…

Of course, I'm referring to the rag-tag force of construction workers, firefighters and cops who had assembled themselves at the site…

Nobody told them to come there, and their were no bosses telling them what to do…

Unlike the Deputy Mayor's contractor buddies, they weren't there looking to get paid…they were trying to help out their fellow New Yorkers in a time of unimaginable horror…

They knew what had to be done…and they tried their damndest to do it…

And, for the next 4 days, they would carry out the rescue operations at the towers pretty much single handed, with minimal outside assistance…

There were about 1,000 people working on the 6 story pile of rubble that had been the WTC…except for the firemen, cops and other city workers, none of them were getting paid one cent to be there…but that did not in any way reduce their dedication to the task at hand, as we'll see in the next chapter…

2

"we will do anything to support our country in this time of tragedy" the volunteers in the pit (September 12, 2001–September 14, 2001)

The Ground Zero volunteers faced a quite daunting task—there was a vast pile of rubble before them, about 120 feet high, covering over 16 acres of ground, composed mainly of twisted steel and chunks of broken concrete, and they had to take it apart...

And they had to do so carefully, since nobody really knew how many folks like Genelle Guzman were trapped under there...one false move could cause a cave in, and crush those they were trying to save...

To make matters worse, the 24,000 gallons of JP 4 kerosene jet fuel from the doomed aircraft had set fire to all the paper and furniture in the towers...and all of that stuff was still burning underneath the pile, making the whole heap a glowing smoking mess...

Still, they persevered...it's not like they felt they had a choice...failure really was not an option here...

The civilian volunteers in the pit were, for the most part, blue collar tradespeople (largely male, and, compared to the city's skilled trades workforce as a whole, disproportionately White)...

Most of them were from the construction trades, in particular ironworkers

Ironworkers work with welding equipment, so they were uniquely qualified to cut apart the twisted steel beams with acetylene torches—early on, a request had been put out for them to come to the site and the Greater New York District Council of Ironworkers had encouraged their members to come to the site...

Other metal trades people who work with welding gear—plumbers, boilermakers, steamfitters ect—had also gone down to the site...

Many other construction workers came as well—in particular laborers and carpenters, since their unions, the New York District Council of Carpenters and Greater New York Building Laborers local 79 had sent organized contingents of workers down to the site...

Many of the laborers and carpenters had cutting torch experience too—especially the demolition laborers, and the dockbuilders—carpenters who do piledriving and waterfront construction...

Heavy equipment was essential to this operation—the city had hastily rounded up every dump truck and earth moving machine they could get—and the unions that represent the folks who drive those machines—Teamsters local 282 and the International Union of Operating Engineers—had sent volunteers down to the site to run them

A large number of workers from Con Edison (the power company that serves NYC) and New York City Transit came down as well...

Among the volunteers from NYC Transit was trackworker Eric Josephson...

He was one of the many workers who came unofficially...

"I schemed to get management to send me to work down there...but I was the last guy in the world they were going to send, because of my reputation..."

So Josephson came on his own time...

"I took the subway as far as I could—I don't think I got past Houston St—and then I walked south and people were converging it was different shades of hardhats and colors of hardhats and safety equipment"

Since it was clear where these folks were going...and the need for their special skils was obvious, the cops, soldiers and federal agents guarding the Canal St security checkpoints made no effort made to interfere with these workers' march to Ground Zero "it was the first time in my life that being an obvious blue collar worker ever got me priviliged access to anything anywhere!!!"

As they got closer, Josephson was taken aback by the devastation…"it was like, you know, bombed out…it was all rubble and smoke all over the place—this glow everywhere—no flames, just a glow…"

By the time Josephson got there, the city had gotten some heavy equipment to assist in debris removal—mostly front end loaders from various city agencies—but the bulk of the work involved hand removal of rubble by the workers…"we just started grabbing rubble and passing it back to the front end loaders"

Buckets were used to remove debris from the pile of rubble…as they were filled, they were passed back along the lines of workers back to the heavy equipment…

Unfortunately, not everything they passed back was rubble…"there were one or two bags—bodybags—that passed my way…not full bags…they weighed 20 or 30 pounds and stunk pretty badly…aside from the stinking of the decaying flesh it smelled like burning styrofoam, I'm not sure why…it was pretty hard to deal with but I passed the bags"

The Ground Zero workers had very little supervision at this point…but that actually made it easier for them to do their jobs…

Josephson was inspired by this "…it struck me that there was so little conversation, we knew what had to be done we didn't need any 'planning meetings'—it was kinda like my vision of what socialism would be like—a real cooperative commonwealth…we had no hierarchy, no bosses, and pretty efficient work was being done…"

When bottlenecks or delays came up, the workers immediately resolved them "all of a sudden we ran out of buckets for the rubble…everybody started shouting 'where's the buckets?!? where's the buckets?!? Where's the fuckin buckets???!!!???' inside of a minute and a half we had buckets…way too many buckets, they actually started to get in the way!"

Outside support started to come in…

Corporate America sent supplies…in particular, bottled water "they had a lot of bottled water, bottled water everywhere—every bottled water company in the country must have sent everything they had…I drank a bunch of those bottled waters"

Charitable groups sent food for the workers "I got a turkey sandwich from the Salvation Army"…

They weren't the only charity there…the Red Cross, which hastily assumed the task of coordinating volunteers and donations from New Yorkers to the Ground Zero rescue operation, set up feeding stations for the workers that would be on the site for the rest of the job…

And unions from across the city took responsibility for supplying the workers with safety equipment…

Josephson's union, Transport Workers Union local 100, sent a vehicle full of supplies down to the site…"my union, and a lot of other unions, like the Operating Engineers and the Carpenters, sent these vans—'union mobiles'—I think that's when [local 100 President Roger] Toussaint came to Ground Zero—local 100 and the other unions gave out respirators and sandwiches and union literature (most of which had little or nothing to do with what was going on at Ground Zero—it's just what they had in the vans)"

Safety equipment was as desperately needed as it was in short supply at the site—where, due to their haste to rescue the trapped and recover the bodies of the dead, workers took risks they'd never normally take on their regular jobs…

"The second day, I was in a position so dangerous that I would NEVER work in such a dangerous position for the Authority—I was on the edge of a deep crater, with one foot on a piece of rubble that was kinda stable and the other foot on another piece of rubble that was kinda stable…with those two pieces of rubble spread about a foot and a half apart"

"all of the safe spots were taken"

The firefighters took some of the biggest risks of all…

Which is not really that surprising…

For the firefighters this rescue job was VERY personal (the FDNY is notorious for it's nepotistic hiring—so many of the firefighters were looking for close relatives—fathers looking for sons, nephews looking for uncles, cousins trying to rescue cousins ect)

Many of them worked without respirators—in part because the best way to find unburied dead bodies concealed by rubble is through smelling the odor of decomposition, and you can't smell anything with a respirator on your face—and took extraordinary risks...

Most of the rescues of live survivors were of firefighters involved in the rescue operation who'd gotten buried under unstable debris...

This was also a very personal operation for Roger Lee and the other Port Authority carpenters on the site (and they were among the few tradespeople being paid for their hard work on this job)

Ironically enough, had the towers not been destroyed, they would have been fired—the complex's new owner, Larry Silverstein, had planned to lay them all off, and replace them with lower paid handymen (who made $ 17/hr as opposed to the carpenters $ 40/hr and had a much cheaper benefit package)

On Thursday, September 13, rescuers finally reached Ginelle Guzman...The 31 year old Port Authority clerk was freed from the rubble where she'd been buried alive for over 27 hours, and was immediately rushed off to Bellvue Hospital for medical attention

The bodies of the two firemen who'd shared the small dark crawlspace with Guzman for so many hours followed almost the same route she did, they went across the street from Bellvue, to the Office of the City Medical Examiner—the NYC city coroner...

That lucky young mom was the last live survivor of the World Trade Center bombing to be rescued...

After that point, the Ground Zero rescue mission became what folks in the search and rescue business euphamistically call a 'recovery operation'...

In plain English...a search for dead bodies...

By this point, the city had a somewhat better idea of just HOW MANY dead bodies there would be...

The early estimates had been very very very high...

By midweek, all the companies who had workers in the towers had published lists of their missing employees...

A number of the construction unions had released names of members who they believed had been in the WTC and who were unaccounted for...

The city released preliminary numbers on the number of missing firefighters and other city workers...

The FAA, United and American had released passenger lists as well (with the names of the suspected terrorists carefully seperated from those of their innocent victims)

And, since the towers were a WORLD trade center, a number of foreign consulates in New York released lists of their missing citizens...

There was some overlap here—the consular lists included a number of folks who were counted by their employers, and the construction union lists included several firefighters who were ex-construction workers but still had paid up union cards...but the number was a lot lower than the early estimates (6,000, rather than 20,000)

That number would be reduced down even futher as time went on...first to 3,600, and then again to 2,900, which would become the final official death toll estimate

Also, to help with the gruesome but necessary task of collecting DNA samples (since most of the human remains coming out of the site were in small mangled pieces, rather than whole bodies), the city set up a sample collection center...

Initially, the Office of the City Medical Examiner used New York University Medical Center—just up the street from the city morgue on E 34th St...

The small space the medical examiner's office secured at the hospital soon became overwhelmed with waves of grieving relatives...

Also, it may have been felt that the NYU Medical Center site was just a little too close to the parking lot where those 26 refrigerated tractor trailer trucks that United Parcel Service had donated to OCME were idling…

Why make the familes walk past trailers full of the mangled remains of their loved ones??

Especially if they might just catch a glimpse of soldiers loading the trucks with small foul smelling plastic bags that used to be people?

So OCME moved to bigger quarters at the National Guard Armory on East 25th St and Lexington Av…a larger space that was far away from those UPS trucks and their gruesome human cargo…

Within days, the operation was moved again, to an even more spacious location—Pier 94 at the Passenger Ship Terminal on the West Side Highway at W 54th St…

Relatives were told to come with hairbrushes, toothbrushes, dirty laundry or any other item that might contain DNA of their missing loved ones…in the case of blood relatives (in particular, mothers and daughters) they were also urged to leave DNA samples of their own…

The reason OCME preferred DNA from female relatives was simple genetics—those samples would be genetically closer to the missing person than those from male family members…

Family members were also asked about any identifying marks—dental work, tattoos, scars, breast implants, circumcision, body piercings ect—that might help the medical examiners identify the family member's remains…

And, the New York County Surrogates Court had folks on hand to assist relatives in filing what are technically known as "affidavit death certificates"—so people could file for their benefits and insurance claims before the bodies got found and identified…

The coroner's office wasn't the only public agency that set up it's Ground Zero operations along the West Side Highway

The US Navy had sent the aircraft carrier USS George Washington, along with a task force of 5 surface warships and a troopship full of Marines, to provide air cover for the city—in case of some kind of second wave of attacks…

Attached to the fleet was the USNHS Comfort, a hospital ship, which docked at the Passenger Ship Terminal, while the combat ships lay offshore…

There were no injured survivors for the Navy Medical Corps folks to assist…but they were able to provide extra manpower down at Ground Zero…

The FBI also set up camp in the West Side Piers—they took over the mothballed former US Navy aircraft carrier USS Intrepid, the centerpiece of the Intrepid Sea Air and Space Museum, as a forward operations base for the 4,000 agents they rushed to the city…

Just down the road, the New York State Police and the New York State National Guard took over the Jacob K. Javits Convention Center…

The center had been abandoned by both trade show workers and exhibitors during the attacks (a trade show had been moving in—the booths were left half-built when all the people fled in terror after the towers fell)

The State Police had a longstanding presence at the center (they'd come in back in 1995 as part of a move to drive out Genovese family gangsters from the Javits—and they still had a barracks deep in the bowels of the vast building)—so it was a logical place for the troopers and the national guardspeople to set up base camp…

But all the state troopers, federal agents and military personnel were merely suppliments to the city's 40,000 strong police department, and the 11,257 city firefighters who had lived through the bombing…

The FDNY had it's personnel on 48 hour shifts—24 hours in their home firehouses, and 24 hours in the pit…

The NYPD, while not as Ground Zero-focused as the FDNY, had all of it's officers on 12 hour shifts—in practice, many worked round the clock, in particular those who were being rotated through Ground Zero or the Frozen Zone and Security Zone checkpoints…

But, while various public agencies were hard at work, the city's vast private sector economy had screeched to a halt...

The bombing had effectively shut down the city's economy—close to half a million people had worked in the Security Zone area (which still stretched from 14th St to the southern tip of Manhattan at that time) and many of them were home jobless...

The sealing off of the Frozen Zone and the Security Zone had in effect shut down the 3rd largest central business district in the United States

Most importantly, the New York Stock Exchange, the American Stock Exchange and the Commodity Exchange had been shut down for days...(in the Commodity Exchange's case, their offices, trading floor and below ground level vault in 4 World Trade Center had been destroyed in the attacks—the building was actually still on fire at that time)

Also, every construction site in Manhattan below 59th St had been shut down since Tuesday morning, putting many of the city's 200,000 construction workers on the unemployment line...

The closing of the airports had shut down the city's tourism business...laying off tens of thousands of hotel, restaurant and bar workers...not to mention the thousands of workers at JFK, La Guardia and Newark airports...

And, the conversion of the city's main convention center, the Javits Center, into an emergency barracks for the National Guard and State Police had idled almost 2,000 carpenters, teamsters and housekeepers...

Similarly, the redeployment of the West Side Piers as a disaster relief center had idled the hundreds of longshoremen who normally worked there...

The city, state and Red Cross set up emergency financial assistance programs (they ended up in the West Side Piers too)

They were mainly focused on helping the families of the workers killled in the bombing, but also offering help to those rendered jobless by the attacks...

But, that state of affairs couldn't go on for very long...

The city had to get back to work...

Even if it meant reopening offices in the area contaminated by the suicide attacks long before they could be properly cleaned (or, in most cases, without them getting really decontaminated at all)…

That also meant repairing the buildings near the old WTC site as quickly as possible too…again, with safety considerations put by the wayside…

Of course, with the buildings near Ground Zero (and, of course, the pit itself) there were other issues that would have to be disregarded as well…

Like criminal investigation and human remains recovery…

Ground Zero was, after all, a crime scene—there had been mutiple felonies committed on that 16 acre site—two incidents of air piracy that had resulted in 2,900 homicides and the destruction by arson of 9 very large buildings…

If the Ground Zero site, and the damaged buildings immediately around it, were to be carefully searched and investigated by trained bomb squad detectives, fire marshals, Bureau of Alcohol Tobacco and Firearms agents and military personnel, it would take literally years before the area could be redeveloped…

Years of lost revenue for Larry Silverstein and the Port Authority…

And that just would not do…

Those buildings had to be rushed back on line ASAP…

There was another reason for not conducting a serious investigation—there was money to be made from the debris itself—in particular, the hundreds of tons of steel in the World Trade Center's beams…

Much of the world's steel industry uses scrap metal as a raw material—and they pay good money for high quality scrap…

In the case of the World Trade Center debris not only was it top-of-the-line structural steel, there was an awful lot of material to be had…

Some of the larger beams weighed as much as 1,400lbs/ft…and there were a hell of a lot of those beams in the pit…

In the construction business in New York, scrap metal (commonly known by the Italian slang expression "mongo") is a much sought after commodity...

And there was a hell of a lot of mongo to be had at Ground Zero...

Bottom line, if the WTC's steel beams were held as evidence, the Port Authority and Silverstein would not be able to recoup their losses by selling all that mongo for scrap...

With these money matters in mind (and all other considerations—investigation, worker safety, recovery of 9/11 victim's remains—secondary at best), a series of decisions were made in the days after the air raid that would affect the rest of the Ground Zero job...

First of all, instead of the site being under the jurisdiction of the Fire Department—the entity that investigates all fires and building collapses in New York City—the site was handed over to the Department of Design and Construction, a city agency that builds police precincts, firehouses and other public buildings...

DDC in turn hired 4 private contractors, Turner Construction, AMEC, Bovis Lend Lease and Tully Construction to supervise the removal of the debris...

DDC divided up the security zone around Ground Zero into sectors for the contractors:

Turner got Seven World Trade Center plus the area from Vesey St north to Chambers St and from Broadway west to the Battery Park City Esplanade...

AMEC got Tower 1, Tower 6, part of Tower 5, the northwestern corner of Austin J. Tobin Plaza, the American Express Tower, 4 World Financial Center and the Crystal Pavillion...

Bovis Lend-Lease got Tower 2, the southwestern corner of Austin J. Tobin Plaza, the Marriott World Trade Center, 90 West St, the (still intact) Marriott Financial Center, 1 World Financial Center, 2 World Financial Center, Gateway Plaza and the North Cove yacht basin...

And Tully got the rest of Tower 5, Tower 4, the eastern half of Austin J. Tobin Plaza, the Deutsche Bank Building plus the area from Broadway east to Washington St and from Vesey St south to Rector St...

A number of trucking companies and heavy construction contractors would use dump trucks to haul the debris out of Ground Zero, and a tugboat company called Weeks Marine would handle shipping much of the scrap metal and other debris away from Lower Manhattan and to the Fresh Kills Landfill in Staten Island—where it could be hauled away to be melted down for scrap...

DDC decided behind closed doors which companies they would pick—no other firms were invited to offer their services...

DDC did not require the contractors they picked to offer any kind of set price for the job—basically, they'd bill the city every week for how much money they'd paid in wages and material costs and the city would pay them...

As I've said earlier, this is highly unusual in the construction business, especially for a job of this size and complexity—for the crudely simple reason that this method of pricing invites fraud by the contractors...

No background checks were performed on either the 4 prime contractors or any of their subcontractors (in some cases, firms specifically barred from doing city work due to alleged organized crime ties were given contracts—this was especially true of the firms supplying the dump trucks)

To expedite the demolition process, the volunteers would be removed from the site as quickly as possible, and replaced by hired employees of the contractors...

There were some semilegitimate reasons for removing the volunteers...

Like civil liability—after all, this was probably the most dangerous jobsite in the world, and, sooner or later, somebody would get hurt and down the line that would guarantee lawsuits would get filed...better to have employees that were workers comp covered than volunteers who were not...

Also, this was a crime scene, and needed to be properly secured—having random folks coming in the site was not such a good idea...

Already, the ranks of the volunteers had been infiltraded by paparazzi seeking gruesome photos of the devistation and looters seeking to rummage through the abandoned stores (and even to rob the bodies of the dead)...so site access needed to be secured...

Of course, those arguments could have been used to justify having detectives, federal agents, fire marshals and soldiers do the cleanup—instead of construction workers with no crime scene or body recovery training...

Of course, construction workers (in particular New York construction workers—the most productive tradespeople on the planet) DO have one type of training that cops, soldiers and firefighters do not...

They're trained to get their jobs done as quickly as possible...

Apparently, that was the priority here...

Once the volunteers were out, and had been replaced by hired construction workers, the push would be on to get the site cleaned out as fast as possible...

The people of New York City (and the Ground Zero workers) would be told that this was to make sure that the families got their loved ones bodies back as soon as possible...

As I've just explained, that was far from the truth...

Now, all of these companies are under contract with the various construction unions, and they would use 100% union labor on this job...(more or less)

But, the unions would do their part too...

And not just at the WTC site...

Citywide, construction unions ordered all their members who'd been employed on 9/11 to return to their jobsites (the New York District Council of Carpenters actually told the workers it was their "patriotic duty" to go back to work building offices!!!)

At Ground Zero itself, Bovis, Turner, AMEC and Tully would be allowed to ignore various union rules—for instance, what construction unions call "jurisdiction"

That is, requirements that particular types of work can only be done by folks from certain unions, for instance, only operating engineers can use cranes or bulldozers, or only carpenters can build or take down scaffolds ect...

Without those rules, contractors would tend to use lower paid workers in place of higher paid ones (for instance, $ 27/hr laborers in place of $ 40/hr carpenters)

Also, despite the physical dangers of the job, (not to mention the psychological toll of working around dead bodies every day) it would be run with as small a crew as possible, and with those workers on two 12 hour shifts (7AM to 7PM and 7PM to 7AM) there would also be a 7 day work week (in the New York construction business, we call this kind of schedule "7/12s")

This would allow the contractors to get the most amount of work done with the least amount of manpower…

Running a job like this on a schedule like that pretty much guranteed there would be lots of injuries in the short term and, due to the heavily polluted nature of the site, lots of job related diseases in the long run…

And that's basically what happened…

But, first, the volunteers had to be removed…

At 11:59PM Friday September 14th, the volunteers were told that they would be provided with a late dinner in the Red Cross feeding center in the Marriott Financial Center hotel…

They got their food…and were then told that they could NOT return to the site…

Tully, Turner, AMEC and Bovis had send their paid workers to the site in place of the volunteers—their role in the job was over…

3

"...on a time and materials basis" from recovery operation to fast track demolition job (September 15, 2001–May 30, 2002)

AMEC, Bovis Lend Lease, Turner Construction and Tully Construction deployed their first workers on the Ground Zero site at 12:01 AM Saturday, September 15...

The crews were largely composed of structural ironworkers and laborers, reinforced by a large fleet of operating engineer-run excavating machines and front end loaders and many many many teamster-driven dump trucks hauling away all of the debris...

There were folks from other trades there as well—in particular carpenters—but mainly the workforce in the pit was composed of those with demolition-related skills...this job was all about cutting up rubble (and whatever else—including more than a few body parts) and shipping it out...As Soon As Possible...

The vast majority of the workers on scene at this point—but a few of the volunteers had managed to evade ejection from the site...

In particular, guys who had not been on duty at midnight, when the contractors came in and the volunteers were lured off site with the promise of a free dinner at the Marriott Financial Center Hotel, were still trying to get to the pit and work...

At least one of those volunteers, ironworker Joe Picurro, actually managed to stay at Groud Zero for another 4 weeks…(he would later pay dearly for his generosity, as we'll see below)

Trackworker Eric Josephson tried to get back to the pit…unsuccessfully…

It was hard for Josephson to even get to Ground Zero "…on Saturday [September 15] it became a LOT harder to get through the barricades—I talked my way through—on condition that I immediately report to the National Guard command post on West St to get a Ground Zero ID"

Once inside the Frozen Zone, Josephson wasn't even allowed to work "I was detailed to wait in a tent, to await work assignment from a fire chief"

"I kept asking him 'do they need me yet?' and he kept saying 'not yet"

"'do they need me yet?"

"'not yet"

"'do they need me yet?'

"'not yet"

"Finally the chief said 'nobody needs you today and we're probably not going to need you at all…cause we're trying to keep track of things down here'"

There was no more need for volunteers…at least not in the pit

"there was no work for me in the pit—only for the professionals—so I was deputized to staff the [Transport Workers Union local 100] van and I handed out respirators…"

That would be Josephson's last day at Ground Zero…

As the last of the volunteers were being eased out of Ground Zero, one of the employee construction workers trying to keep track of things down there in the pit was carpenter Christopher Caches…

He was the foreman of a crew that was cutting up big steel beams into pieces small enough to be hauled away…

Caches is what is known in the New York construction business as a "company man"—that is, he gets his jobs directly from the contractors, rather than through the union…

This job was no exception—and he'd even gotten them to hire his son as well…

Caches also, like many company men, occasionally worked for less than union scale in return for steady employment (a practice union carpenters call "working for cash") and this job was no exception as well…

But, this was not a normal job for Caches…"I was running a cutting gang—about 8 guys and me—and we burned through this big beam…After we cut it, we had the crane lift it up—and there was this thing underneath it…it was somebody's rib cage…just a rib cage, nothing else"

Seeing that kind of stuff, day after day after day, soon took a mental toll on the normally cheerful and happy-go-lucky Caches…"after about two weeks, I told my son 'this job is not for you…you gotta leave here' I made him quit the job"

"A couple weeks after that—I had to leave too…I couldn't take it anymore"

"You know, I can understand why they bombed the Pentagon—that's a military target—I don't think it was right but I can understand it…but this was a civilian building…why did they have to attack here???"

Port Authority carpenter foreman Roger Lee also saw a lot of stuff in the pit that people really should never see "…ya know, they kept this out of the papers, cause they didn't want to hurt the families, or mess up guys' death benefits…but, a lot of the Port Authority cops we pulled out of the rubble had shot themselves in the head…"

"They'd been trapped, and didn't think they were ever going to get rescued, so they took out their guns and shot themselves"

Needless to say, seeing stuff like that, 12 hours a day, day after day after day, took a severe psychological toll on the Ground Zero construction workers…

Not to mention the physical effects…

The site was still on fire, and toxic fumes were being constantly released…

And not just the smoke from the burning furniture and paper…

When Seven World Trade Center fell, it destroyed the huge Con Edison electrial transformer station in it's basement…

That tranformer station was filled with polychlorinated biphenyls [PCB's]—an extremely toxic chemical commonly used as an insulator in high voltage electrical equipment…

All those PCB's got released into the air when the transformer blew…

PCB's are a known carcinogen—that is, exposure to them is likely to give you cancer…

Speaking of cancer-causing substances, the WTC was one of the last major buildings in the United States that was insulated with asbestos…the year the WTC was finished—1972—was the year that asbestos was outlawed in this country…

Much of that asbestos had been removed—but by no means all…

There was enough asbestos in the towers when they fell that, weeks later, some nearby offices contaminated with World Trade Center dust had an asbestos count as high as 369 fibers per cubic centimeter of air…

For those unfamiliar with asbestos, that's high…

Very high…

Superfund high…

Seal off the building and call in the folks with the moonsuits and respirators high…

Normally, if the asbestos count is above 10 fibers per cubic centimeter of air, a full decontamination job is required…

Monokote—the insulation spray, made from chemically treated recycled newspaper, that was used to replace the asbestos was also released into the air when the towers fell

Monokote isn't quite as bad as asbestos—but, as any carpenter or plasterer who's worked with that stuff knows, it has it's own hazards—it's a skin, eye and lung irritant…

And that's just from having a little bit of it fall on you while you're working around it…

When the towers fell, 220 floors worth of monokote insulation got dispersed into the atmosphere…

Fiberglass, the main component of the insulation in the walls of the WTC (and every other building in the city with metal framed sheetrock interior walls) also got released into the air as the buildings disentegrated—and that's an eye, skin and lung irritant too…

Speaking of sheetrock, the most harmful component of World Trade Center dust was the raw material that sheetrock is made from…gypsum—which is also one of the main raw materials of the concrete in the complex's core walls and floor decks…

When all that concrete and sheetrock got pulverized, all that gypsum turned into a fine easily inhalable dust…

The clouds that enveloped all of Lower Manhattan when the towers fell—the stuff people referred to as "smoke" was in fact gypsum dust, produced by the breaking up of all those concrete decks and sheetrock walls…

Anybody who's ever worked in construction knows just how much dust concrete and sheetrock produce, even in small amounts…and just how irritating that dust can be to the mucous membranes of the nose, throat and lungs…

Now, what we had here is what scientists would call "synergistic effects"—that is, as bad as all this nasty stuff (smoke, kerosene fumes, PCB's, asbestos, monokote, gypsum ect) were as seperate substances, their poisonous effects would be far far far worse once they were mixed together into a breathable toxic stew…

It should go without saying that any area covered with this stuff would be a very toxic zone, that would need to be properly cleaned…

And WTC dust was dangerous stuff—there were office workers who had athsma who died on the spot when they were enveloped by the clouds as the towers fell…

The evident danger was clear…

However, there were factors far more important that safety at stake here…

Of course, I'm talking about the billions of dollars in losses caused by the WTC attack—an estimated $ 60 billion dollars in projected insurance claims (the largest "insurable event" in the history of the world up to that time—only Hurricane Katrina 5 years later would eclipse it) and the billions of dollars being lost EVERY DAY that the Financial District was shut down…

In light of that fact, US Environmental Protection Agency Administrator Christine Todd Whitman announced that the air was safe in Lower Manhattan—and the reopening of the Financial District began…

Along with debris clearance, the four contractors began to hire subcontractors to clean out the non destroyed buildings on the edge of Ground Zero…

Of course, many of these buildings were far from occupiable at this point…

First step was getting the lights back on…(since it would be extremely difficult to repair the buildings without electricity—and impossible for the office workers to go back to their jobs without power)

Con Edison had it's workers out on the streets of Lower Manhattan working night and day to get the power back…and, with destroyed below ground power lines replaced by temporary open air electrical cables running through the gutters, the power was soon restored…

Then phone service would have to be restored (cause office workers cannot do their jobs without voice and data communication)…

Verizon had armies of telephone workers on the job around the clock, rebuilding the Verizon Building (with the aid of large numbers of construction workers) and restoring the cables under the streets…

The telephone workers toiled under horrible conditions—the Verizon Building had no running water or toilets, and in many places it didn't even have exterior walls anymore (which is not a very safe thing when you're 20 or 30 floors above street level)

With the lights on and dial tones restored it was time to replace all the broken windows…

AMEC, Bovis, Turner and Tully had put up plywood to temporarily seal up the buildings—but that would not do…there was no way that office workers could be persuaded to work under those conditions…

So, architectural metal & glass contractors were hired and they brought in several hundred carpenters, glaziers and ironworkers to replace the windows (which in many cases involved putting in new window frames as well)

Even at this early date, there were subtle signs that these were far from normal construction jobs…

When this writer got a call from the New York District Council of Carpenters Out of Work List to go to a job replacing raised floor panels in the Verizon Building, I was told that this assignment was "strictly on a volunteer basis—you don't have to take it if you don't want it…you'll still keep your spot on the list…"

Normally, if a carpenter refuses a work call from the NYDCofC Out of Work List, for any reason, no matter how legitimate (even if they have to take their kid to the hospital), he/she immediately gets kicked off the list, and has to put his/her name on the bottom of the list (which in mid September 2001 would mean they'd have 3,000 guys and gals ahead of them on the list)…

For some odd reason that was NOT the case here…

Perhaps the District Council had some idea of just how dangerous these sites were, and didn't want any future liability lawsuits from members forced to take jobs there??

In any case, they didn't explain WHY you could turn these jobs down…

I took the hint, if they're letting us refuse these jobs, their MUST be some extraordinary hazard down there…so I refused the call (I didn't make it down there for several more months—when the site had become far less dangerous)

Once the buildings had their exteriors sealed, their interiors had to be cleaned out (many of the buildings were filled with thick layers of World Trade Center dust)

Normally, cleaning out toxic potentially asbestos containing material (or ACM, as it's known in the abatement business) is work that is performed by highly trained abatement workers—highly trained laborers with special licenses from the city and state to handle highly toxic material…

One little problem…

In New York, most of those laborers are union members (represented by local 78 of the Laborers Union) and they make $ 25.50 in wages and $ 6.81 in benefits per hour…

That's a lot of money…especially since much of the work would have to be done on overtime (local 78 doesn't have that many members—and there were a lot of buildings that had to be decontaminated)

Also, local 78 laborers work under strict safety conditions—

The contractors they work for have to have air samples from the jobsites laboratory tested on a regular basis…

Also the workers are protected by special respirators and disposable moonsuits when they work, elaborate 'negative air pressure' ventilation systems to remove the dirty air from the job and replace it with clean air, jobsite showers so the workers can clean themselves before lunch and at the end of the workday, and regular medical examinations to check them for cancer and lung diseases, paid for by the employer…

All that safety adds up…especially since the showers are built by $ 40/hr carpenters and the ventilation systems are set up and run by $ 27/hr operating engineers…

On the other hand, the building owners of Lower Manhattan and the four Ground Zero contractors had a much cheaper option…

When the towers were blown up, 1,100 janitors instantly lost their jobs…

Unlike most of the office workers at the towers (most of whom were kept on the payroll while they were awaiting reassignment to alternative locations), the building maintenance workers got laid off as soon as the buildings collapsed

The union that represented those workers (Service Employees International Union local 32B-32J) spoke to their former employer—American Building Maintenance [ABM] about new job assignments...

ABM promised the union that they had temporary jobs for each and every one of these workers...either on ABM's payroll, or working for One Source, another large unionized janitorial contractor...

On the surface this sounded like a great deal...

But there was a catch that ABM kinda forgot to mention...

The temp jobs would involve cleaning out the World Trade Center dust from the contaminated buildings around Ground Zero...

Unlike the abatement laborers, these janitors would not have special respirators (the lucky ones got 99 cent store dust masks—some folks didn't even get that, they had to tie rags or handkerchiefs around their faces)

There would be no special ventilation...nor would the cleanup sites be sealed off from the outside world to prevent the toxic material from spreading...

There would be no disposable moonsuits, nor would their be showers on site—so the workers would have to carry the toxic dust on their workclothes and their bodies onto the subway and back to their homes...

Worse yet, these workers would be doing a $ 25.50/hr job for only $ 9/hr...

A pretty good deal for the building owners...

And a massive screwjob for the workers...

Laborers local 78 strongly objected to the use of lower paid Service Employees International Union janitors to do their members jobs...

But, amazingly enough, SEIU local 32B-32J took ABM and One Source's side in this dispute...the union defended the contractors using their members as untrained cheap labor on these extremely hazardous jobs...

In the end, local 32B-32J, ABM and One Source won…and the workers were sent to clean toxic waste for only $ 9 bucks an hour with only 99 cent store dust masks standing between them and terminal diseases…

Sad to say, the local 32B-32J janitors didn't have it the worst…

Milro Services, a non union janitorial contractor from Freeport, Long Island, had it's janitors working side by side with the SEIU-represented office cleaners from ABM and One Source…

Milro's regular employees were back on the Island, so they set up a streetcorner labor shapeup at the corner of Broadway and Fulton St to hire local workers…

During the early days of the cleanup, they'd hire a crew of about 100 workers every morning, and then march them as a group through the checkpoints (since most of their workers were undocumented Latino immigrants, most of whom did not have any kind of ID, that was the only way they could get them through security)

Milro paid it's workers $ 60 bucks for an 8 hour shift, or $ 90 bucks for 12 hours…that works out to $ 7.50 an hour…

Needless to say, they did NOT get time and a half for overtime…

Since they were paid off the books, they did not get any kind of benefits—no social security, no workers compensation coverage, no unemployment insurance, no nothing…

The absence of any kind of payroll records also could be used to evade any responsibility for workplace injuries (a loophole that Milro would take advantage of later on)

Many of them didn't even get paid (Milro had a nasty habit of missing pay-days—knowing full well that their illegal immigrant workers wouldn't dare call the Labor Department)

There were actually workers who were worse off than the folks at Milro…

Many of the rich people who lived in the luxury apartment houses of Battery Park City used their low paid undocumented immigrant servants to clean their homes…

Some hired day laborers to help out their cleaning ladies…

It's hard to say exactly how badly most of these workers were paid, due to the fact that most of them were paid off the books, with no social security, workers compensation, unemployment or disability benefit premiums paid…

It should almost go without saying that none of these workers had health coverage…

Like the janitors, the maids and day laborers had no special training in handling toxic waste…and no employer supplied protective equipment (not even dust masks) and no medical monitoring of the health effects of their exposure to the dust…

This had predictable results…

An estimated 400 janitors and day laborers would suffer injuries during the course of the cleanup operation…and, as we'll see below, many more would get sick from the toxic dust they breathed in…

They weren't the only workers at risk…

Many restaurants, delis and retail stores in the area used their regular workers to clean up the WTC dust—for their regular pay (but, usually, the bosses did pay for the dust masks)

Beyond the worker safety issue, quite naturally, the cleanups done by unskilled workers without proper equipment were slipshod, at best…

Basically, visible dust got removed—but contamination hidden inside airducts, below raised floors, above ceiling tiles and in other hard-to-reach spots stayed where it was (in some places, there's probably some WTC dust still there today)

As the surface dust was washed away, office workers were rushed back to their desks…

Like Khadija Lawrence—who was ordered to go back to work 2 weeks after the attacks—even though her office at Getty Images was so close to Ground Zero that she could smell the pit's distinctively horrible odor "…like burned plastic and burned meat—like you put a steak in the frying pan without takin it outta the package first"

And Fady Mitchell, who "…had to go back after 3 weeks, with all that stink and all that smoke"…

But the child support collection offices at 2 Washington St weren't nearly as sanitized as the Administration for Children Services claimed—"they didn't half clean up the building…some of that stuff is still up there now, up in the ceiling tiles…"

But not every worker could be sent back into the contaminated zone so quickly…

The buildings closest to the pit couldn't get those kind of quick and dirty cleanups—there was just too much internal damage…

So, many of the office towers in the Security Zone around Ground Zero got their interiors completely demoed out…

They were among the few offices in Lower Manhattan that got anything remotely resembling a proper cleanup

Even then, the contractors used the lowest paid workers they could get away with…

Instead of specially trained $ 25.50/hr hazmat laborers from Laborers local 78 (the only folks in the city who were actually trained to do this kind of work), the contractors used $ 17/hr demolition laborers from Laborers local 79…

The local 79 demolition workers, besides making $ 8.50 an hour less in wages, also didn't have the same training as the men and women from local 78…They also lacked the costly safety protections—respirators, moonsuits, decontamination showers, special ventilation systems, regular medical screening…

In other words, these cleanup jobs were done quick, cheap and dirty too…

Two buildings never got taken care of (and still sit there as bombed out husks to this very day)…the Deutsche Bank Building on Liberty St & Greenwich St, and Borough of Manhattan Community College's Fitterman Hall on Vesey St and Greenwich St…

These are both fairly large structures—Deutsche Bank is a 50 story skyscraper, and the BMCC building is 14 floors high…

And they were both pretty badly screwed up…Deutsche got hit by pieces of Flight 11 and was impaled by major structural elements of Tower 1 and got scorched by a major fire…Fitterman got clipped by a major section of Tower 2…

They were unrebuildable, and it was decided that they had to be torn down…

Unfortunately, that was easier said than done…

None of the engineers could figure out a way to take them down without recontaminating the whole area around the two buildings…That was a major problem, with Deutsche on the south side of Ground Zero, and Fitterman on the north, that would basically negate the whole cleanup job…

So, after a cursory search for dead bodies, the buildings were left standing…

Meanwhile, back in the pit, the demolition job continued at a fast clip…

One of the major priorities was tearing down Tower 4…

That lowrise building had survived the bombing (more or less—it also got gutted by fire after Tower 2 fell)…but the problem was what lay beneath the ruined 6 story low rise office building…

Tower 4 had been home to the Commodity Exchange…

And, among the commodities traded there were silver and gold…

As it happened, a pretty sizable amount of the silver and gold that was brought and sold in the exchange was physically in Tower 4…in an extremely large vault operated by a Canadian financial servics firm, the Bank of Nova Scotia…reportedly, there was about a half billion dollars worth of precious metal underneath the building…

$ 500 million in gold and silver being a lot more important than finding human remains for proper burial (at least in the minds of the folks from DDC who were running the job) taking down Tower 4, and removing the valuables from the basement, suddenly became very important…

Tower 4 was demolished with great speed…

When the vault level was reached, a large force of well armed federal agents were dispatched to that portion of the site, to seal the area off…

Once the vault was reached, the feds waited until the 7PM shift change—and once the day shift were gone, almost all of the night shift were given the evening off—except for a few ironworkers, laborers and operating engineers—just enough guys to get the massive vault opened up…

As the doors were burned off, a fleet of armored cars was assembled—the money transporting vehicles were then moved in, one at a time, to take out the gold and silver…

This gold and silver recovery operation was carried out with great care and coordination…

The same could not be said for the human remains recovery operation…

Basically, by this point DDC, the contractors and Mr Silverstein wanted the site demoed as soon as possible…with minimal regard for remains recovery…

The one major obstacle to this was the large contingent of firemen working on remains recovery detail in the pit…

The city had reduced the size of that force—down to only 75 firefighters per shift, working alongside a 75 police officer detail drawn from NYPD and PAPD detectives…

But, even with a greatly reduced strength, the firefighters tended to slow down the demolition operations…

Huge excavating machines, designed to tear up dumptruck-loads of debris with only a few scoops of their powerful mechanical arms, were slowed down to a snail's pace—one scoop at a time, with many stops for the firefighters to go in with rakes to sort through the debris for bodies and body parts…

And that just would not do…

After all, Larry Silverstein had a building to build…and he was still paying $ 1.2 million a month in rent on the 7 towers that had gotten blown up…

Time is money…and the firemen were wasting a lot of Mr Silverstein's money by taking time to properly search for the bodies of the dead…

So, on October 30, Mayor Giuliani announced that 2/3rds of the firemen would be pulled out of the pit…

The excuse was 'safety' (a jawdroppingly bogus explanation—as we've seen, nobody in authority really gave a damn about Ground Zero worker safety)

The far more likely reason—the simple fact that it's really hard to do a fast track demolition job when an investigation is in progress, so the investigative personnel had to be pulled out to push the job…

Needless to say, this enraged the firemen, many of whom were looking for the bodies of their murdered relatives…

Remember, in the nepotism-ridden FDNY, most firemen are related by blood and/or marrage to other members of the department…

Some guys actually came out of retirement to find the bodies of their sons…

So being asked to abandon the remains of their relatives (or, worse yet, consign them to being dumped in the Fresh Kills Landfill with the other debris) was unacceptable…

And the way the firemen got asked inflamed tempers too…

FDNY Commissioner Tom Von Essen, when told of the firefighters heartfelt objections to the new plan, told them to "suck it up and take it!!!"…

Ironically enough, Von Essen used to be the PRESIDENT OF THE FIRE-MEN'S UNION, which made his offensive outburst that much harder to take…

The union Commissioner Von Essen used to run, the Uniformed Firefighters Association, tried to calm the firemen down while attempting to negotiate a continued FDNY presence in the pit, but, within a couple of days, the union had to accomidate the anger of their members…

So, on Thursday November 2, the UFA called a rally a few blocks from the pit…

They tried to keep the workers away from the site, but the firemen walked away from the official rally and marched on Ground Zero...

The construction workers in the pit responded to the firemen's wildcat strike with a work stoppage of their own—with some ironworkers actually joining the firemen's rally

The New York Police Department responded with nightsticks and handcuffs, attacking their fellow uniformed city workers and placing 12 of them (including the presidents of both the UFA and the Uniformed Fire Officers Association) under arrest...

DDC did attempt to identify, and blacklist, the ironworkers who participated in the firemen's wildcat...

Commissioner Holden sent out his official photographer to take pictures of the workers who had joined the firemen in their wildcat, but he ended up backing down from firing those guys, apparently due to fear a jobsite wide walkout of all the other trades if those militant ironworkers got kicked off the job...

There were other concerns too...

The general election was just 5 days away...

Giuliani couldn't run again...but he was supporting Republican candidate Mike Bloomberg...

Bloomberg, in turn, was depending on getting crossover Democrat votes to win election...in particular, the votes of firefighters and unionized construction workers...

This would be a horrible time to antagonize those voters...

So the city abandoned it's plan to fire striking ironworkers at Ground Zero...

The city also backed down on it's plan to reduce the number of firemen in the pit—the four contractors would just have to work around them...

DDC did remove most of the detectives—they were sent out to Fresh Kills landfill, to inspect the rubble for pieces of dead bodies as it was unloaded from the barges...

Unlike a typical NYPD crime scene operation, where all evidence is carefully catalogued, this was a production job, with speed far more important than a proper investigation…

Many of the detectives at Fresh Kills literally worked on an assembly line, rapidly checking the rubble as it went via conveyer belt from barge to landfill…hoping that they could spot a piece of flesh or a bone fragment before it was interred forever in the huge city garbage dump…

Needless to say, that setup was far from ideal for a proper investigation…

It did help move the job along a whole hell of a lot faster…steel beams were being pulled out, temporary roads had been built, the "bathtub" (the large foundation wall that kept the World Trade Center foundation hole from being flooded by the Hudson River) was being shored up and the partially flooded PATH train tunnels to New Jersey were being pumped out and repaired…

The job was taking a lot faster than anybody thought (of course, with all the inconvenient and time consuming investigative stuff brought to a halt, and those slowpoke firemen and detectives pushed out of the way, the construction workers could be pushed to work at the high speed that New York City tradespeople customarily perform our jobs at)

This did lead to some accidents…quite a few of them actually…

Even though Turner, Tully, Bovis and AMEC were claiming this was the "safest large jobsite in the world", there were an estimated 5,000 worker injuries during the course of the Ground Zero recovery operation…

Most of these were comparitively minor (at least by construction standards)…

The four contractors systematically downplayed all but the most major of injuries—in some cases, badly hurt workers were told to come to the site, and got paid, even though they were too hurt to work, just to conceal the actual numbers of injuries on the site…

As for the civil servants, 500 firefighters who were hurt at Ground Zero put in for disability pensions in the first few months after the attack…

This massive toll doesn't even include all the folks who got sick from the dust, or the mental effects of seeing all the horrible stuff in the pit…we'll talk about them later on…

As the pit got rapidly cleaned out, there was some conflict on the management side…

There was the whole ugly matter of how Tully, Turner, AMEC and Bovis got this job, apparently using their patronage hookups to lock out other contractors…

Bechtel, Inc. was one of those companies, and they wanted to get in on the action…

And the San Francisco-based heavy construction giant, the largest general contractor in the world, actually had a legit case…

Among the firm's many specialties, they actually did battle damage remediation (they did a lot of the rebuilding work after the Iran Iraq War)

Tully Construction, a road paving company from Queens, didn't have that kind of experience…neither did office building construction general contractors Turner, Bovis Lend Lease or AMEC…

And Bechtel was 100% American-owned, unlike the German-owned Turner Construction, and the British-owned Bovis Lend Lease and AMEC…

However qualified they were, Bechtel simply didn't have the kind of City Hall patronage hookups that Turner, Tully, Bovis and AMEC had…

The four contractors used their media contacts to brand Bechtel an "out of town company"

That's a truly bizarre claim, since three of the four Ground Zero contractors were European-owned firms…

The four contractors also got the unions on their side, getting them to claim falsely, that all the unionized tradespeople would get laid off and Bechtel would run the job non union…

Of course, Bechtel is an 'open shop' contractor…union in some places, scab in others…but then again, so are Bovis, AMEC and Turner…

Both Bovis Lend Lease and AMEC run non union jobs back home in England…

And Bovis, AMEC, Turner and Bechtel alike all work scab when they operate in Saudi Arabia and the Persian Gulf states (since unions are illegal over there)

But, in New York City, Bechtel was 100% union (and was actually running a large union job in Midtown Manhattan at the time—they were renovating Penn Station for the Long Island Rail Road)

Beyond the red herring labor and "out of town company" issues, Bechtel WOULD have saved the New York City taxpayer a bundle…

They would have billed the job the regular way (ie put in a bid and got paid a fixed amount—rather than the open ended T & M setup that the four companies had)

And their costs would be a lot lower…

Among other things, they'd only have one set of managers to pay, rather than the 4 sets of bosses that the other companies had to take care of…

Also, Bechtel actually knew how to run jobs in war zones…unlike these firms…

But, Bechtel didn't know anybody in City Hall, and Bovis, Turner, Tully and AMEC did…

So the four companies kept the job…and kept sending in their T & M tickets every week and getting their big fat checks from DDC…

During this whole controversy, New York City got a new mayor…

Rudy Giuliani's second term expired (and in New York, public officials are only allowed to hold two consecutive terms of office)…

Media billionare Mike Bloomberg, one of the 500 richest guys on the face of the earth, had planned to run as a Democrat, but he turned Republican to evade a hard primary…

As a Democrat, Bloomberg would have faced off against former consumer advocate Mark Green and Bronx Borough President Fernando Ferrer...

As a Republican, his only opponent was former East Harlem congressman turned corporate lobbyist Herman Badillo...whom Mike (and his oceans of money) easily beat in the primary...(a primary which was stopped on 9/11 and rescheduled 2 weeks later)

Billionare Bloomberg easily beat Green—the winner of the Democratic primary—in the general election (his money helped here too...and the fact that Green had alienated Black and Latino Democrats by waging a racially charged campaign against Ferrer—and the fact that a racially insensitive legal brief Green wrote back when he was a student at Harvard Law School was exposed in the media just a couple days before the election)

Bloomberg was sworn into office New Year's Day 2002...

Rudy Giuliani went into business for himself, starting a consulting firm called Giuliani Partners...he specialized in advising cities on reorganizing their police departments to make mass arrests of poor people...

Former Commissioner Kerik, a specialist in that department, went to work for Rudy...

One of Kerik's first jobs was helping reorganize the Mexico City Police Department along NYPD lines...and training them how to wage police terror in the ghettos by making lots of petty arrests of poor inner city minorities (in Mexico City's case, the minority group to be persecuted were Mexican Indians)

Former Deputy Mayor Rudy Washington, who had been the top city official at Ground Zero, was now out of a job (New York City mayors appoint their Deputy Mayors—and they leave their jobs when the mayor who appointed them leaves office) had intended to use the private sector to cash in on his former official post too...

A former drywall contractor, he would have been in a perfect position to cash in on those $ 7 billion dollars in no-bid contracts he'd authorized in the pit, and get himself a nice job with a big fat salary from one of the contractors he'd assisted...

One little problem...

Ironically, Deputy Mayor Washington's decision to run the Ground Zero job quick and dirty had boomeranged on him...

Deputy Mayor Washington had caught a bad case of World Trade Center Cough...and was unable to work...

For the time being, Bloomberg left Commissioner Ken Holden in charge of DDC, and Deputy Commissioner Mike Burton stayed on in the pit...(actually, Burton had a lot more responsibility now—unlike his predecessor, Bloomberg didn't have a deputy mayor on site full time, so the deputy commissioner was now the highest ranking public official in Ground Zero)

Meanwhile, back on the jobsite, on the perimiter of the pit, in the Ground Zero Security Zone, the repair jobs on the buildings surrounding the pit moved rapidly forward...

With the exception of Fitterman Hall and the Deutsche Bank Building, all of the office buildings on the edge of the pit had their interior demolition completed...

With the contaminated areas demoed out, interior construction operations could rapidly moving forward...electricians put in new wiring, carpenters framed out and sheetrocked walls, and installed ceilings, floors, woodwork and interior partition systems, tapers and painters finished walls, steamfitters put in new sprinkler systems and convectors, sheet metal workers installed new airducts and the laborers swept up behind everybody else...

These jobsites were actually kinda normal (as long as you didn't look out the windows facing the pit and watch the firemen raking up the debris for human remains)

These jobs did have an abnormal amount of security around them...there were a lot of checkpoints, and toolbags got searched by security guards when you entered a building, it was really hard to even get to work, since all the nearby subway stops had been blown to bits during the air raid and there were lots of semibogus "safety" requirements, like making workers wear hardhats on interior construction jobs...

By the time this writer arrived in the Ground Zero Security Zone (April 19, 2002—almost at the end of the job) it was almost 'normal'—at least outside the pit...

The stench had long since died down, and almost all of the dust was gone…

Other than all the checkpoints (and that huge hole in the ground where the WTC used to be) you'd almost think it was a regular job…

I was sent to be the carpenter shop steward for a furniture installation contractor, L & D Installers, replacing the office furniture in the executive floors of the American Express Towers, at 3 World Financial Center…

A big part of our job involved installing new desks in the offices of Chairman Kenneth Chennault (he actually came to the site one day, and shook the hand of all the guys and gals working on the 51st Floor "thank you, you're doing a good job")

American Express Towers had been pretty throughly cleaned up—you'd never know that all the windows on the eastern elevation of the building had been blown out, or that a big chunk of the building had been ripped open by the fall of Tower 1, or that 11 people had died in the building or that the whole interior had been coated with dust or that the local 79 demolition laborers had to rip out everything and put it in the dumpsters…

American Express was fixed up nicely enough that the folks from DDC moved out of PS 89 and put their temporary offices there…(apparently, they got tired of sitting in those little kid-sized chairs with the desks attached to them)

One of L & D's project managers claimed to me that "they got $ 500 million from the insurance company to clean up this building—but they only spent $ 100 million"…

One day, standing on the 51st floor balcony at breaktime (watching the firemen rake up the dust in the pit to find body parts), he also told me that "see where we're standing right here?…when they first got here, they found a bunch of bone fragments right here"

But, what really made it clear that this was not a regular job was when we went downstairs for lunch…

A lot of Battery Park City was back to normal—the delis were open, and you could even play video games in this game room area of 3 WFC's atrium…

There was a movie theater right by our site—Robert De Niro had launched a film festival, to bring tourists back to Lower Manhattan, and it was going on right during the time we were working…

One day at lunchtime, one of the workers for the Tribeca Film Festival offered us free tickets to a movie…We would have taken her up on her offer—but, unfortunately we had to go back to work at 12:30…

Things may have seemed almost normal here…even though we were within site of the pit

But, in a big white circus tent-type structure in the parking lot north of Battery Park City's movie theater, the Red Cross still had their Ground Zero worker feeding station set up…

These really friendly folks from the Midwest served up hot food (it wasn't really cooked that well…their pasta dishes in particular tended to really suck…but hey, it was FREE, right, so who's complaining???)

Looking around at the tables, you could tell, pretty much at a glance, who was in the pit, and who was in the security zone…

The guys on the building renovation jobs in the security zone acted just like regular construction workers at lunchtime—laughing and joking, or just quietly enjoying their food…

But for the guys from the pit…it was a whole different story…

They looked really really really sad—ESPECIALLY the firemen…

Many of them had this odd kind of look about them, like they were spaced out or something (what this writer's father, an ex-Marine, probably would have called a "ten thousand yard stare")

You'd see this "ten thousand yard stare" most commonly among the firemen

They'd be sitting there, in their modified uniforms (they had regular fireman helmets, and blue FDNY shirts with their company insignia on the front, but they had on brown Carhartt overalls and workboots, instead of the 'bunker gear' insulated raincoats and pants they usually wear) and most of them looked really really really messed up…

Which makes perfect sense…

How would YOU feel if you were digging up the bodies of your cousins or brothers-in-law????

Probably about as bad as these guys did…

In any case, the job was coming to a close…

My job got finished on May 15…and the guys across West St in the pit were pretty close to done too…

All the structural steel and other rubble was gone, and the site had been cleared all the way down to the bedrock…

Within two weeks, on Thursday, May 30, the Ground Zero job was officially finished…

A little ceremony was held—kinda like the "topping out parties" that general contractors have when they finish building the top floor of a building—of course in this case, it was the reverse (a "bottoming out party", perhaps?)

For obvious reasons, this event was a lot more somber than your average topping out event…(no free T-shirts, sandwiches and beers here)

AMEC, Bovis Lend Lease, Turner Construction and Tully Construction walked away from this job $ 7 billion dollars richer…

A new general contractor, Tishman Construction, was brought in to build the Freedom Tower, Seven World Trade Center, the other two office buildings and the new PATH train station…

Ironically enough, Tishman had been the general contractor that built the old WTC back in the day…

The crew was cut down to a much smaller workforce, just enough guys to do the foundation work for the new towers to come, and to rebuild the Port Authority train station…

The "heroes of Ground Zero" had finished their service to their city and their country…

But their battle had only begun…

4

"...your claim for benefits is hereby rejected" who will help the 'heroes of Ground Zero'??? (May 30, 2002–)

On Wednesday, September 29, 2004, 2nd year apprentice carpenter Winston Thomlinson made history...in a bad way...

The 29 year old Jamaican immigrant became the first worker to die at Ground Zero...(or at least the first Ground Zero worker to actually die on the jobsite itself—there were other job related fatalities going on—but they were disease-based and happened off site)

Thomlinson was working on the new Seven World Trade Center...

This was the first of Larry Silverstein's new buildings (paid for by his insurance double dipping—the courts had approved his attempt to get $ 6.6 billion off a $ 3.3 billion policy—proving that you can get away with just about anything if your rich enough)

Silverstein was in a big hurry to get these towers up...after all, he still had to pay the Port Authority their $ 1.2 milion dollars a month rent, no matter what...

So, the general contractor, Tishman Construction, was pushing it's subcontractors...

And the subcontractors in turn were pushing their workers...

Nowhere was this more true than with Prince Carpentry, the drywall subcontractor for the job…

Prince has a 40 year long ugly reputation among union carpenters in New York—the company is notorious for abusing it's workers (in particular it's carpenter apprentices) and forcing them to work at a brutally fast pace…

Tishman was pushing Prince to get the "core work" done…that is, the drywall in the elevator shafts, around the "service core" of the building (the area where the elevators, fire stairs, bathrooms and chase walls for electrical, heat and plumbing systems are located) and around the outer perimiter walls…

Once the core work is done, it is then possible to do the "tenant work"—installing the drywall partitions and interior systems for the companies who will be moving in to the offices…

There was a small problem here…there were no tenants to be had…

The 50 story tower was empty except for the 2 floors to be occupied by Silverstein Properties (the two LOWEST office floors—cause Mr Silverstein is not a dumb guy and wanted to hedge his bets in case of a possible future terrorist attack—low floors tend to be the easiest to escape from in case of disaster)

Be that as it may, Mr Silverstein still wanted his building done on time…the sooner the project was done, the sooner he could try and get tenants in

September 29 was an especially fast paced day on this job…

The New York construction unions had scheduled a labor rally that day…

The theme was not the horrendous worker safety conditions on New York jobsites, or the fact that 70% of the construction in the city was done non union…

Instead, the unions were trying to drum up public support for giving $ 600 million dollars in public subsidies to floorwax billionare Robert Wood Johnson IV, the owner of the New York Jets…

The floor polish dude wanted a brand new stadium (even though he had a perfectly good one just across the river in New Jersey)…but Robert IV (who prefers to be called "Woody") didn't want to pay for it—he felt that working class New Yorkers should give him a stadium, for free…

For some sick reason, the New York construction unions agreed to support this vulgar money grab by one of the richest men in the country…and they felt that other working class New Yorkers should support it too…

That's why the called the rally…

As is customary, workers at these rallies get paid for the day (as long as they work part of the day) and they often get free T-shirts, baseball caps and, sometimes, they get free food too…

So there was a big rush on many jobsites to get as much work done as possible before lunch, so the workers could get to the rally…

Knowing Prince, they quite possibly expected a full 7 hour day's worth of work to be done before lunchtime…

If true, this no doubt posed a serious problem for Thomlinson…

As is customary at Prince Carpentry, the hardest jobs were assigned to the least skilled carpenters, the apprentices…

Thomlinson had been told to put wood planks in an elevator shaft, so "coreboard" (inch thick, 2 foot wide and 8 foot long pieces of sheetrock, designed to be fireproof and often used to insulate elevator shafts and other core areas of buildings) could be installed…

This is a very risky job—do it wrong and whoever goes out on those planks is at high risk of falling to their deaths…

Journeylevel carpenters should be doing that kind of stuff…but they might be inclined to take their time and do it right…

Apprentices on the other hand, being young, inexperienced and anxious to make a good impression on their foreman (cause that could lead to a "company man" spot, the closest thing in our industry to a steady full time job), would tend to go out there and do the job fast and dirty…even though it puts their lives at risk…

That's apparently what happened to Thomlinson out in that elevator shaft…

Something went wrong, and the apprentice fell 16 stories to his death…

When he hit the elevator pit, he was so mangled that Prince's foremen could only identify him by rounding up every carpenter on their crew, counting heads and figuring out who the dead guy was by process of elimination (that is, since he was the only guy on their crew who was not in the shanty, he must be the dead guy at the bottom of the shaft)

Pretty grim stuff, but it gets worse…

Winston Thomlinson joined local 157 of the Carpenters Union in 2002…

Had he joined before 1995, Thomlinson's family would have been elegible for $ 10,000 in death benefits from local 157's parent union, the United Brotherhood of Carpenters and Joiners of America…

But, in that year, the new "reform" leaders of the UBCJA phased out death benefits for all new members…abandoning a 114 year old union policy of guaranteeing that every union carpenter got a decent burial (ESPECIALLY carpenters who died on the job)

Since Thomlinson's family was poor, they had no money for a funeral…and since he had just joined the union, he wasn't elegible for that $ 10k benefit…

Local 157 ended up having to send a memo to every shop steward in the local (and forwarding copies of that memo to the other 9 Carpenters Union locals in the city) asking them to pass the hat, so the union could give money to Thomlinson's sister to pay for a decent burial…

In the end, Mr Silverstein got his building…on time and on budget…

He didn't have any tenants (other than his own company, and Con Edison, who has a humongous electrical transformer that takes up the first 10 floors of the tower), but he's got a building…

It's really pretty too…a lot nicer looking than the old Seven World Trade Center…

And it's got a whole bunch of fancy features—including elevators with no buttons (building security automatically programs the cars to take you to the floor you're supposed to go to)

But, was it really worth Winston Thomlinson's life???

As we've seen, in the minds of the folks who run this city, workers lives really aren't that valued when there's a lot of money at stake…

We'll see this point illustrated in greater detail below…

As for the Ground Zero job itself…at the time of Thomlinson's death just about the only things that had been accomplished in the 2 1/2 years since the Ground Zero recovery job officially ended were the rebuilding of the PATH train station and the construction of Tower Seven…

The Deutsche Bank Building and BMCC's Fitterman Hall were still standing, pretty much in the same state of delapidation they'd been in since the day the buildings fell…

Deutsche Bank had been surrounded by scaffolding, and sidewalk bridges at street level—but the engineers still hadn't figured out how to tear it down without contaminating every other building between Liberty St and the Brooklyn Battery Tunnel…

Worse yet, the contractor hired to tear down Deutsche, Safway Environmental, was an extremely dirty firm, even by the very low standards of the demolition industry…

Safway allegedly had mob ties, a horrendous safety record (even by demolition business standards—and that's saying something) and an awful EPA record (again, that's awful by the awesomely low standards of the demolition business)

Also, there were still body parts in and around Deutsche, and a proper search had still not been done (at this writing, in late July 2006, they're still finding human remains in that building)

Fitterman had similar problems…three contractors bid on the job…and they were all as dirty as Safway…so no reputable company could be found to tear the building down…

Also, if Fitterman Hall was demoed the wrong way, it would contaminate the newly built Seven World Trade Center (just about the only building in the area that was 100% clean)

There was also an awful lot of political wranglilng over the 3 other buildings that Silverstein was supposed to build—who'd pay for them, who'd build them, who'd rent them out once they were built ect…

There was a four way battle for control over the site, between the City of New York, the State of New York, the Port Authority of New York/New Jersey and Silverstein Properties…

There was also a long running dispute between the families of the dead and those 4 entities over exactly what type of memorial would be built over the site…

Even among the victims families, there was a factional split—between the relatives of the civillian workers and the families of the firefighters—over how the victim's names would be placed on the memorial wall…

Also, the NYPD was fighting with the architects of the new World Trade Center over making the buildings safe from the likely reality that there will be a future terrorist attack on the new towers…

Basically, the police want a lot of safety features that will cost Mr Silverstein a lot of money…and, of course, Mr Silverstein does NOT want to spend that money…

Foundation work for the Freedom Tower didn't even start until 2006, due to all the political wrangling (and the ugly reality that the tower doesn't have any tenants)

And there was a problem with that…

Mr Silverstein had Tishman Construction, his general contractor on Seven World Trade Center, act as his GC on Freedom Tower…

And they hired a contractor called Laquila to do the concrete work…

One very big problem…

Laquila has issues…major issues…

The company is barred from working on any city jobs…and Laquila's trucks are barred from hauling garbage in the city…due to alleged mob ties…

And those allegations are pretty serious…

Gambino family captain Michael "Mickey Scars" De Leonardo testified under oath that when Laquila's owner, Dino Thomassetti, Sr, first got in the New York concrete business in 1968, he paid $ 75,000 in tribute to the Gambinos to be allowed to do hirise concrete work in New York City…

Mickey Scars further alleges that, for many years afterward, Laquila paid $ 10,000 a month in tribute to the Gambinos and the Colombo family to be allowed to stay in the concrete business…

Further, it has long been alleged by law enforcement that Laquila had ties to alleged Gambino family member Edward Garafola and to alleged Colombo family member Ralph Scopo…

Scopo was a pretty important dude in the concrete business…he was the head of the Laborers Union's Cement and Concrete Workers District Council, the union that represented all the unionized concrete laborers in New York City and Long Island…

As concrete laborers are the largest group of workers employed by concrete contractors, having an "understanding" with Scopo could allow a contractor to carry out all sorts of labor abuses, with no fear of Laborers Union sanction…

Scopo could also make sure that, if a contractor wanted to use laborers to do the jobs of higher paid carpenters, cement masons, ironworkers or operating engineers, those unions would not object to the practice (even though it cost their members job opportunities)

Speaking of labor abuses against operating engineers, Laquila has also been indicted for allegedly bribing officers of the International Union of Operating Engineers, so that union's $ 46/hr heavy equipment operators can be replaced with $ 31/hr concrete laborers on Laquila's jobsites…

The alleged relationship with the Gambinos also reportedly helped Laquila dump it's construction debris in an illegal dump, rather than having to pay high prices at a regulated sanitary landfill…

Beyond the allegations of 38 years of gangsterism, Laquila has a history of sub par performance…

Back in 1995, Donald Trump hired Laquila and another hirise concrete contractor, North Berry, Inc, to do the concrete work at Trump Riverside South…

It was set up as a competition—Laquila got one building, North Berry got another one…

The company that did the best job would get the remaning 12 buildings (a decade long job)…come in second and you'd get thrown off the job…

Laquila came in second…

A distant distant distant second…

In their haste to get the floors poured, they used the thin mix concrete, intended for the floor decks, in the columns, and the thick concrete, needed to make the columns strong enough to support the weight of the building, was poured on the decks…

This was unacceptable—not to mention dangerous—and, at considerable expense, Laquila had to chop out the weak columns and repair them with grout…

As a result of that screwup, Mr Trump will not use Laquila on any of his future jobs…

North Berry [since renamed Northside Construction] got the rest of the Trump Riverside South job…a job they're still working on to this day

This is the company that Mr Silverstein picked to do the concrete for the Freedom Tower.

But, due to the sensitive legal issue of Laquila being banned from government work, an elaborate subterfuge had to be set up…

Dino Thomassetti Sr had one of his kids, his 27 year old son Dino Jr, act as his faceman on this job…

Dino the younger, who's only previous work experience is being his dad's chauffeur, set up a front company (also called Laquila—in this case Laquila Group) to run the Ground Zero job…

One of Thomassetti Sr's top executives, Angelo Sisca, is actually running the job day to day (possibly because of Dino Jr's gross lack of any real construction experience)

Dino Jr's trucks are all registered to his dad's company (supposedly they were "donated") and they're painted in the exact same green with red trim and LAQUILA written in white letters on the sides color scheme as his father's vehicles...and he has the same office at 1590 Troy Av in Brooklyn, and even the exact same phone number, as his dad's similarly named firm...

Thomassetti Sr, who isn't even allowed to visit the site, due to his longstanding record, has all of his kids involved in this setup—his 40 year old son Rocco's firm Empire Transit Mix is supplying the concrete and his 39 year old daughter Elaine T. Scotto's company, J & E Industries, is supplying the steel rebar...

But, according to Mr Silverstein, all is well...

Silverstein Properties has hired an ex federal prosecutor, Thomas D. Thatcher, as the "integrity contractor" for the job...

Apparently, Mr Silverstein's firm cannot do "integrity" in-house, so they have to subcontract it...

This is not a good sign for how the rest of this job will go...

While Larry Silverstein was trying to buy himself some integrity, thousands of Ground Zero workers were getting sick, many were dying, and nobody wanted to compensate them...

As I mentioned above, during the course of the job, about 5,000 construction workers and 400 janitors suffered injuries during the course of the cleanup operation...

Most of those were minor, and almost all of those workers quickly recovered...

However, within just a few months, the long term effects of exposure to World Trade Center dust began to present themselves...

The occupational medical specialists at Mt Sinai Medical Center (who have been monitoring Ground Zero worker health since shortly after the attacks) discovered that many workers in and around the pit had serious respiratory problems...

The doctors felt this was a brand new disease, and gave it a name…

World Trade Center Cough…

In 2002, under pressure from the doctors at Mt Sinai, the NYC Department of Health & Mental Hygene set up a World Trade Center Health Registry, to monitor the physical and mental health problems of Ground Zero workers…

Over 71,000 people (including this writer) have registered with them…

Examining the reports from the folks who signed up with the registry, the people from the Health Department soon made a very alarming discovery—many many workers at Ground Zero had gotten chronically ill…

Unlike most occupational illnesses, which take years to appear, World Trade Center diseases rapidly showed symptoms…

And it wasn't just coughing and reduced lung capacity…

Many Ground Zero workers had cancer—often exotic, not easilably treatable varieties of that disease…and in many cases, the tumors were very agressive…

These workers urgently needed assistance, both medical and financial (since many had become too ill to work)

Unfortunately, that help was NOT forthcoming…

The "heroes of Ground Zero" were going to get stiffed…

Like ironworker Joe Picurro…

We met him above, a volunteer who came to the site, and unlike most of the volunteers, who got kicked off the job the first weekend after the disaster, he stuck around for 28 days, working without pay…

Picurrro developed respiratory problems, and filed for workers comp in 2004…

And he got denied by the New York State Workers Compensation Board…

He applied again…

And got denied again…

And he applied again…

And got denied again

Picurro, who can barely speak anymore (let alone being able to handle heavy structural steel and welding equipment on jobsites) was told that his application was "flawed" and that he could not prove he was even at Ground Zero…

This was even though Picurro had had the presence of mind to have another worker take some snapshots of him, in his work clothes, in the pit (with the fires of Ground Zero plainly visible in the background)…and he submitted the photos to the board along with his application…

It took two years (and some embarrassing media coverage on Fox News and in the New York Daily News) to get the Workers Compensation Board to reverse their decision…

At this writing, the WCB still hasn't cut Picurro a check…

Picurro's wife Laura fears that the WCB is dragging it's feet for a crassly simple reason…

They are waiting for Joe to die…so they won't have to pay him at all…

And he's not the only ironworker to get cheated out of his benefits…

John Sferazo has permanently scarred lungs, and can no longer work in the trade…

Winston Lodge has chronic bronchitis, acid reflux, constant headaches and nose bleeds, and shortness of breath so bad the doctors actually had to operate on his sinuses so he can breathe…he hasn't been able to work as an ironworker for 4 years…

Joseph Libretti also has scarring of the lungs, and can no longer work…(as well as scars you can't find on an X ray…his brother Daniel, a New York City fireman, died in Tower 1—that's why Joseph spent so many hours searching the debris in the first place)

According to one study, 77% of the ironworkers who worked in the pit have some type of respiratory disease…

Which makes sense...not only did they have the toxic dust, but also the fumes from the welding equipment they used...and the exhaust from the diesel powered heavy equipment all over the site...

Butt wasn't just tradespeople that got sick...

Firemen were the first to suffer job-related illnesses in the pit...

Within 2 days of the terrorist attack, an astonishing 9,000 firemen (out of 11,257 who passed through the pit in that time) suffered from sinus, throat, lung or chest problems...

240 of them had to go to the hospital...

Just two weeks after the attack, a firefighter who worked on the site was diagnosed with interstital lung disease and acute eosinophilic pneumonia—basically, his lungs were filled with fluid and the air sacs in his lungs were damaged...from breathing in a whole lot of toxic dust...

The firemen had to work without respirators—to be able to locate the decomposing bodies by smelling their odor—so their lungs took a beating...

Many police officers also suffered lung injuries for the same reason...

But they wern't the only ones...

Even office workers in nearby building were sickened...

Like Tarnisa Moore, a supervisor at the Marriott World Trade Center Hotel, who now sufferes from athsma and lung disease...

And Fady Mitchell (who we met eariler in this book), who claims that most of her co-workers from ACS are now suffering from World Trade Center related diseases...

Fortunately, she got a transfer to the ACS office in the Queens County Family Court (which caused many of her symptoms to go away)...

Many of Mitchell's co-workers who are still assigned to 2 Washington St are still suffering...

Even the well-to-do folks who live in Battery Park City are suffering…many women in the neighborhood who had children after the attacks reported maternal health problems and/or low birth weight babies…

And, as I mentioned above, former Deputy Mayor Rudy Washington has World Trade Center Cough too…

Unlike the Ground Zero workers, many of whom have been repeatedly denied coverage, the deputy mayor had no problem getting the Workers Compensation Board to approve his case…

I wonder why????

All told, approximately 12,000 men and women who worked in or near the towers are known to be suffering from World Trade Center-related diseases…

57 of those folks have died from their World Trade Center-related diseases…

In four of those deaths—Firefighter Steven Johnson, Police Officer James Godbee, Detective James Zadroga and FDNY Paramedic Debbie Reeve—even the city had to admit their deaths were directly because of their Ground Zero service…

Dr David Prezant, the deputy chief medical officer of the FDNY, has done his own study, confirming that there are widespread WTC-related illnesses among firemen who worked in the pit…

According to the FDNY's Dr Prezant, the average firefighter who worked in the pit suffered the equivilant of 12 years of lung damage during their work at Ground Zero…

Typically, the longer they worked in the pit, the worse their symptoms are now…

Despite this mountain of evidence, the city has refused to come to the workers aid…

Instead, the Corporation Council of the City of New York has used federal World Trade Center disaster funding to pay for the lawyers who fight the Ground Zero workers claims!

White Plains, NY-based personal injury attorney David Worby is in the process of filing a class action claim, on behalf of 8,000 Ground Zero workers and their families…

Unfortunately, many of these workers may no longer be alive when this case finally makes it's way through the court system…

CONCLUSION

◆

The Fire Next Time

The World Trade Center bombing may have been the largest terrorist attack ever to occur on US soil…but it probably won't be the last…

As long as Corporate America continues to enrich itself off of the cheap labor and low priced raw materials of Third World countries, there will be folks in those nations who will want to strike back at their economic exploiters…

And they won't necessarily follow Geneva Convention rules when they attack…

As long as this is the case, American workers will be caught in the crossfire…

In the long run, we as a working class need to do something about that…(basically, we need to replace our present corporate-dominated economic system with one run by the working class)…but that discussion is far beyond the framework of this book…

However, since we will almost certainly be hit again, we need to think about how American workers will react…

No doubt, when the next raid comes, our patriotism will be appealed to…and we will be asked to work under dangerous conditions…to make massive sacrifices in the name of rescuing survivors, recovering the bodies of the dead and "protecting our nation"…

How should we respond??

In particular, how should unionized construction workers respond, since we will be expected to deal with future terrorist attack-caused building collapses

Even now, three building industry unions—the New York District Council of Carpenters, Operating Engineers local 94 and Service Employees International Union local 32B-32J, have their own emergency responder training programs…

Transport Workers Union local 100 has a similar program for their members, run by a former Israeli secret police agent…

This is exactly what we should NOT be doing…

It's very understandable that, during and immediately after an attack, construction workers will rush to the scene of a bombing-related building collapse, to help the firefighters and cops rescue survivors…

In the chaos that almost invariably happens in the wake of a surprise attack, we might just be the only folks out there capable of getting the job done…

And, if lives are at stake, we should be in there trying to safe people…

Unfortunately, this will almost certainly lead to injuries, illnesses and even deaths from among our ranks…

That's exactly why our position should be that we should not be in the anti-terrorism response business…

Once the cops, federal agents, firefighters and military personnel have established a perimeter, and more importantly once it's clear that there are no more live survivors to be rescued, there should be very few, if any, of us behind their barricades…

Our demand should be that the attack-affected area should be kept sealed off until it is completely decontaminated…

As long as their is an active crime scene (that is, until the fire marshals and detectives have removed all the bodies, and gathered all the evidence) we simply shouldn't be there…

It's not our job…and, as we have seen with Ground Zero, if we get sick or die we will not be compensated…

Once the evidence has been cleared and the bodies recovered, only workers who are trained and equipped to handle toxic waste should be anywhere near the site…

Regular construction workers should not be down there until it's completely safe…

And, under no circumstances should untrained near-minimum wage janitors and day laborers be used in place of skilled hazmat abatement laborers…that's just wrong…

Of course, if a future terrorist attack affects a major central business district and or a very important public building (like 9/11 did) we'll be under enormous pressure from the business community—and the government they control—to go in and get the site cleaned up quick, cheap and dirty, so they can get back to business ASAP…

People like Larry Silverstein will tell us it's our "patriotic duty" to get their buildings back into rentable condition immediately…and the folks who run our unions will be tripping all over themselves to agree!!!

The main lesson of September 11th for New York construction workers is that we were used as corporate pawns…our heroism and civic mindedness was used against us…

We risked our lives…and our heroism was cynically abused to benefit the money-men…

Our patriotism was twisted and distorted…to line the pockets of Larry Silverstein and the owners of Tully Construction, Turner Construction, AMEC and Bovis Lend Lease…

In the process, our skill and productivity was perverted to destroy many of the very human remains we sought to recover…

Along the way, we unwittingly helped Mr Silverstein and the scrap dealers destroy the evidence of why the towers fell so quickly…just so he could make a few million dollars selling the mongo to sweatshop steel mills in India, China and Turkey…

That evidence might have saved future workers from dying in building collapses…but now we'll never know…

Worst of all, now that many of us are sick and dying—our health broken to enrich Mr Silverstein and the contractors—and they don't even want to give us that paltry little $ 405 a week in workers comp!!!!

The "heroes of Ground Zero" are now treated like homeless beggars on the street!!!

We should NEVER ever let that happen to us again…

978-0-595-40919-8
0-595-40919-9

Printed in the United States
204047BV00002B/65/A

9 780595 409198